START-UP TO SUCCESS

BUSINESSPERSON'S BLUEPRINT

DR. S. THOWSEAF

Made with ♥ on the Notion Press Platform

www.notionpress.com

To my ever-patient family—especially to my spouse,

who endured countless late nights of "just one more chapter,"

and my son, who somehow still believes "business"

is just another word for building forts out of cardboard boxes.

Your unwavering support and occasional reminders to eat something

other than pizza have kept me grounded through this journey.

To my mentors and colleagues, thank you for sharing your wisdom

and for not laughing (too hard) when my ideas sounded more like dreams.

And to every aspiring entrepreneur reading this,

may your dreams be as bold as your morning coffee

and your determination as resilient as Wi-Fi on a stormy day.

CONTENTS

FOREWORD

Welcome to a journey that blends the art of entrepreneurship with the science of success. In these pages, Dr. S. Thowseaf takes you by the hand and guides you through the intricate maze of starting and scaling a business. With a blend of scholarly insight and practical wisdom gained from years in academia and industry, Thowseaf unfolds a narrative that is both enlightening and engaging.

Entrepreneurship is more than a career choice; it's a calling—a journey filled with thrilling highs and inevitable challenges. Through this book, Thowseaf not only equips you with the essential tools and strategies but also injects doses of humor and empathy, reminding us that behind every business plan lies a story of courage, perseverance, and a touch of madness.

As you embark on this adventure, prepare to be inspired, challenged, and entertained. Whether you're a seasoned entrepreneur or a novice dreamer with a laptop and a vision, the insights within these pages will illuminate your path and fortify your resolve. Let's dare to dream big, laugh often, and forge ahead—together.

Mrs. M. Najeetah

PREFACE

Welcome to "Start-Up to Success: Businesspersons Blueprint," a guide designed to navigate the thrilling, often chaotic, and undeniably rewarding journey of entrepreneurship. If you've picked up this book, chances are you've felt that unmistakable spark of an idea, that itch to create something extraordinary, and the determination to see it through despite the odds. This book is your companion, mentor, and cheerleader as you embark on this exhilarating adventure.

Entrepreneurship is not for the faint of heart. It's for the brave, the dreamers, the doers who see possibilities where others see roadblocks. This book is a culmination of experiences, insights, and lessons learned from the trenches of the start-up world. It's a roadmap crafted to guide you from the initial glimmer of inspiration to the pinnacle of business success. And let's be honest, it's also peppered with enough humor to keep you smiling through the inevitable bumps along the way.

The journey begins with finding your passion—a journey inward to discover what truly ignites your spirit. From there, we delve into turning those ideas into reality, crafting a business plan that not only attracts investors but also serves as a solid foundation for your venture. Funding and financial management, often the bane of an entrepreneur's existence, are tackled with practical strategies and a bit of wit to ease the anxiety.

Building and leading a team is where the magic happens. Surrounding yourself with the right talent, creating a culture that fosters innovation and loyalty, and honing your leadership skills are critical steps in scaling your business. And let's not forget the marketing and sales strategies that will propel your brand into the spotlight. This book offers you tools and tactics to build a compelling brand identity, craft irresistible offers, and close sales with finesse.

Product development and launch are the heartbeats of your start-up, and we cover everything from prototyping to handling unexpected challenges with grace and grit. Operations and scaling take you further, ensuring that your processes are efficient and your growth is sustainable. We emphasize resilience and continuous improvement, encouraging you to learn from failures and adapt to a changing landscape.

Finally, future-proofing your business is about looking ahead. It's about anticipating market trends, embracing innovation, and preparing for the unexpected. This book is not just about surviving the entrepreneurial journey; it's about thriving and building a legacy that stands the test of time.

Throughout these pages, you'll find anecdotes that will make you chuckle, quotes that will inspire you, and practical advice that will equip you to tackle each stage of your start-up journey with confidence. This book is a testament to the countless entrepreneurs who have dared to dream big and worked tirelessly to bring those dreams to life. It's a celebration of the spirit of entrepreneurship and a guide to help you navigate your path to success.

So, buckle up and get ready for a ride filled with highs and lows, challenges and triumphs, and a whole lot of learning. Whether you're just starting out or looking to scale your business to new heights, "Start-Up to Success: The Businessperson's Blueprint" is here to support you every step of the way. Let's turn those dreams into reality, one strategic move at a time.

ACKNOWLEDGMENTS

To say this book is a labor of love would be an understatement. It's more like a marathon run barefoot on a beach strewn with Lego pieces. As I reflect on the journey of bringing "Start-Up to Success: The Businessperson's Blueprint" to life, I am overwhelmed with gratitude for the incredible support system that has been my lifeline.

First and foremost, my deepest gratitude to the Almighty. Without divine grace, I would still be stuck at the introduction, probably tweaking the title for the millionth time.

To my parents, Mrs Hameeda and Mr. Sha Nawaz Khan, your unwavering belief in me has been my greatest strength. Your endless patience, encouragement, and occasional reminders to take a break (read: eat something) have been the foundation upon which this book was built.

My wife, Mrs Najeetah, and my son Ubaid Ur Rahid deserve a special mention. Without them, I might have completed this book long before. Between ensuring I took time out to sleep and bribing me with delicious meals, she managed to keep me sane throughout this process. And to my son, Ubaid Ur Rahid, your curiosity and questions about why Daddy was always at his desk were both a delightful distraction and a reminder of why I was doing this in the first place.

To B.S. Abdur Rahman Crescent Institute of Science and Technology, your new KPI that includes book publishing, was the gentle nudge (read: forceful shove) I needed to embark on this writing journey. It's funny how a bit of professional pressure can turn an idea into a tangible product. I'm grateful for the push—it made this book a reality.

My PhD guide, Dr Ayisha Millath from Alagappa University, has been an invaluable mentor. Your guidance in imparting the writing skill has been instrumental. Every piece of advice, every constructive criticism, and every word of encouragement was a step forward in this long, winding path.

To Mrs Chitra, Correspondent of N.S.N schools and follower of Mahatria of Infinitism, your thought-provoking speeches have been a beacon of inspiration. Your words have the power to ignite a spark of creativity and perseverance, and they certainly played a role in the creation of this book.

And of course, a hearty thanks to Mahatria of Infinitism. Your philosophy and speeches provided the thought-provoking insights that kept me grounded and motivated. The wisdom you impart has a way of making the impossible seem possible, and the mundane seem magical.

A special shoutout to my Macha, Mr. Ameerudin, from Elsevier company. Your meticulous help in the review process and your sharp scrutiny were vital. Without your keen eye and attention to detail, this book would have had more plot holes than a block of Swiss cheese.

To everyone who supported me through this journey, thank you. Your encouragement, your patience, and your belief in this project were the fuel that kept the engine running.

This book is a culmination of countless hours of work, sleepless nights, and moments of doubt, but it is also a testament to the power of support, love, and the relentless pursuit of a dream. I am eternally grateful to each and every one of you. Now, on to the next adventure—hopefully, one with fewer Legos on the beach.

I

THE ENTREPRENEURIAL SPARK

PART - I

Introduction

So, you've picked up this book, "Start-up to Success," and you're probably wondering why we're diving into entrepreneurship right off the bat. Well, it's simple: every great start-up begins with the entrepreneurial spark. It's the seed from which all your wildest business dreams can grow. Without understanding the essence of entrepreneurship, we'd be like chefs trying to cook a gourmet meal without knowing what ingredients we need—it would be a disaster.

Think of entrepreneurship as the foundation of a house. You wouldn't start decorating the living room before laying down the foundation, right? Unless, of course, you're into avant-garde living arrangements where the couch floats mysteriously above a dirt pit.

Entrepreneurship is the spark that lights the fire. Picture this: you're at a campfire, surrounded by friends, and someone hands you the job of starting the fire. You strike a match, and voilà, a roaring fire begins. Now, imagine trying to enjoy that campfire experience without ever lighting the match. You'd be sitting in the dark, cold, and probably getting bitten by mosquitoes. It is not exactly the start of a successful evening.

Talking about entrepreneurship first is like kicking off an epic road trip. You need to know where you're starting and have some sense of direction before you hit the gas. Otherwise, you might end up in the middle of nowhere with only a "Welcome to Nowhere" sign and a bewildered expression. Entrepreneurship is that thrilling yet nerve-racking first step where you decide to leave your comfort zone and dive into the great unknown. And hey, who doesn't love a bit of an adventure?

Definition and Significance of Entrepreneurship

Entrepreneurship is like the magical alchemy of the business world. It's the process by which individuals convert brilliant (and sometimes not-so-brilliant) ideas into reality. Simply put, entrepreneurship is the act of starting, managing, and growing a business venture in order to make a profit. But it's much more than that. It's about innovation, solving problems, and creating value in ways that haven't been done before.

Imagine entrepreneurship as a delicious cake. The ingredients are creativity, risk-taking, and perseverance. Mix these well, and you might just end up with a successful business. Of course, there's no guarantee—sometimes you'll bake a dud. But that's part of the adventure.

The Role of Entrepreneurs in the Economy and Society

Entrepreneurs are the superheroes of the modern economy, albeit without capes (usually). They drive economic growth, create jobs, and bring innovation to the forefront. They are the ones who look at a barren landscape and envision a bustling city, who see a problem and develop a solution, who dream big and work hard to make those dreams come true.

Consider this small, humorous story to illustrate:

Once upon a time, in a quaint little village, there lived a man named Joe. Joe was a regular guy with an extraordinary love for cheese. One day, he thought, "What if I could make cheese that sings when you cut it?" (Yes, Joe's ideas were a bit out there). Everyone laughed, but Joe was undeterred. He spent months experimenting in his kitchen. Though he never quite managed to make singing cheese, he did invent a new, delicious type of cheese that quickly became the talk of the town.

Joe's little cheese venture grew, and soon, he was hiring neighbors to help with production and sales. The village thrived, with new shops opening to cater to the increased foot traffic Joe's Cheese House brought in. This whimsical story of Joe highlights the essence of entrepreneurship: turning a unique idea into a reality that benefits not just the entrepreneur but the entire community.

Entrepreneurs like Joe play a pivotal role in society. They create new products and services, spur innovation, and often provide solutions to problems that we didn't even realize we had. Their ventures create jobs, increase competition (which can lead to better prices and quality for consumers), and drive economic growth.

In essence, entrepreneurs are the lifeblood of a vibrant economy. Without them, we'd all be stuck with the same old products and services, and life would be a lot less interesting. So, whether it's creating the next big tech gadget, a revolutionary service, or a quirky new cheese, entrepreneurship is all about making the world a better, more exciting place.

The Birth of an Idea

Every great start-up begins with an idea. But let's be honest: not all ideas are born equal. Some ideas emerge fully formed like Athena springing from Zeus's head. Others are more like a newborn giraffe – awkward, wobbly, and needing a bit of time to find their footing.

Imagine you're in the shower, and suddenly, an idea hits you like a bolt of lightning. You scramble to get out, dripping wet, trying to jot it down before it slips away like soap in a bathtub. That's the thrill of the birth of an idea – it can happen anywhere, anytime.

Sometimes, ideas come from everyday annoyances. Have you ever been so frustrated with a stubborn jar lid that you thought, "There has to be a better way!?" Congratulations, you've just experienced the birth of an idea.

The trick is to recognize these moments and nurture them. Remember, even the mighty oak tree started as a humble acorn.

Identifying the Entrepreneurial Spark

Now that you've got your idea, it's time to identify the entrepreneurial spark. This is the moment you realize your idea has potential – like recognizing your cat might actually be plotting world domination instead of just knocking things off the counter for fun.

The entrepreneurial spark is that little voice in your head saying, "Hey, this could really work!" It's the excitement that keeps you up at night, scribbling notes in the dark because you're too jazzed to sleep.

It's the tingling sensation that tells you you're onto something big.

Identifying this spark is crucial because it's what will fuel your journey. It's the difference between "Eh, maybe someday…" and "Let's do this now!"

If your idea makes your heart race and your imagination soar, you've found your spark. Hold onto it tightly because it's what will propel you forward when the going gets tough.

Inspiration and Motivation

Inspiration and motivation are like the dynamic duo of entrepreneurship. Think Batman and Robin, but with fewer capes and more coffee. Inspiration is what gets you started, and motivation is what keeps you going when you hit those inevitable bumps in the road.

Inspiration can come from anywhere – a sunset, a book, a random conversation with a stranger. It's the spark that ignites your creativity and sets your imagination ablaze. But let's not forget that inspiration can also come from less glamorous sources. Maybe you're inspired by the fact that your last attempt at making pancakes ended in a minor kitchen fire, and you're determined to create a foolproof pancake mix. Hey, whatever works!

Motivation, on the other hand, is what keeps your fire burning long after the initial spark. It's the fuel that drives you to push through late nights, early mornings, and countless rejections. It's the vision of success that keeps you focused, even when your friends are out having fun, and you're stuck at your desk.

To stay motivated, surround yourself with reminders of why you started this journey. Create a vision board, set achievable goals, and celebrate your wins – no matter how small. And when things get tough, remember why you fell in love with your idea in the first place. Your passion is your greatest motivator.

Let's throw in a little humor to keep things light. Picture this: You're at a motivational seminar, and the speaker asks, "What motivates you?" People shoutout things like "Success!" and "Making a difference!" Then, there's Carl in the back, who yells, "Pizza!" Everyone laughs, but Carl's onto something. Sometimes, motivation can be as simple as promising yourself a reward – like a slice of your favorite pizza – after you hit a milestone.

So, as you embark on this entrepreneurial adventure, remember: ideas can be born anywhere, the spark is what sets them apart, and a little humor and motivation (or pizza) can go a long way. Get ready to turn your idea into a success story worth telling.

The Entrepreneurial Mindset

The entrepreneurial mindset is like wearing a pair of glasses that allow you to see opportunities where others see obstacles. It's about being optimistic, resilient, and a little bit crazy – in the best possible way. Entrepreneurs don't just think outside the box; they wonder why there's a box in the first place.

Imagine you're trying to build a sandcastle at the beach, but every time you start, a wave comes and washes it away. The average person might give up and go for a swim instead. An entrepreneur, however, sees this as a chance to build a better sandcastle – maybe even one with a moat that diverts the waves.

Key Traits of the Entrepreneurial Mindset

- Optimism: Entrepreneurs are the kind of people who see the silver lining in every cloud. Remember when the lemonade stand ran out of lemons? They'd probably start selling lemon-scented air fresheners instead. As Henry Ford said, "Whether you think you can or think you can't, you're right" (Ford, H.).

- Resilience: Bouncing back from failure is essential. As the saying goes, "Fall 7 times, stand up 8" (Japanese Proverb). Entrepreneurs understand that each failure is just a stepping stone to success.

- Creativity: Seeing possibilities where others see problems. Think of Thomas Edison, who said, "I have not failed. I've just found 10,000 ways that won't work" (Edison, T.).

- Risk-taking: Entrepreneurs are comfortable with taking calculated risks. It's not about jumping off a cliff and hoping for the best; it's about knowing there's a parachute packed in your backpack.

Embracing the Entrepreneurial Mindset

To truly embrace this mindset, you have to be willing to look at the world through a different lens. You'll start to see opportunities everywhere – from the way people complain about their morning commute to the inefficiencies in their daily routines.

The Art of Opportunity Recognition

Recognizing an opportunity is a bit like playing "Where's Waldo?" but instead of finding a guy in a striped shirt, you're spotting potential business ideas. Entrepreneurs have a knack for identifying gaps in the market and envisioning solutions to problems.

Stay Curious and Observant

- Listen to Complaints: Where there's a complaint, there's a potential business. If you've ever heard someone say, "I wish there was a better way to do this," you might just be onto something.

- Analyze Trends: Keep an eye on industry trends and emerging technologies. The next big opportunity could be hiding in the latest tech breakthrough or societal shift.

- Network: Surround yourself with diverse people who can provide different perspectives. Sometimes, the best ideas come from a casual conversation with someone outside your industry.

Take the story of Sara Blakely, the founder of Spanx. She turned a personal frustration with pantyhose into a billion-dollar empire. She famously said, "Failure is not the outcome – failure is not trying" (Blakely, S.). Imagine if she had just continued to grumble about her hosiery woes instead of seeing it as a golden opportunity!

Turning Passion into Action

Passion is the fuel that drives entrepreneurs. It's what gets you out of bed in the morning and keeps you working late into the night. But passion alone isn't enough – you need to channel it into action.

- Set Clear Goals: Break down your big vision into smaller, actionable steps. As Tony Robbins says, "Setting goals is the first step in turning the invisible into the visible" (Robbins, T.).

- Create a Plan: Develop a roadmap that outlines how you'll achieve your goals. Include milestones to track your progress and stay motivated.

- Take the First Step: The hardest part is often starting. Don't let fear or doubt hold you back. Remember, "The journey of a thousand miles begins with one step" (Lao Tzu).

A Story of Passion and Action: Consider the story of Walt Disney. He was passionate about creating a place where both children and adults could enjoy magical experiences. Despite numerous setbacks, including being told his idea for Disneyland was "too risky," Disney pressed on. His passion turned into action, and the result? It is one of the most beloved entertainment empires in the world. As Disney himself said, "All our dreams can come true if we have the courage to pursue them" (Disney, W.).

Embracing the entrepreneurial mindset, recognizing opportunities, and turning passion into action are the cornerstones of any successful start-up journey. With a bit of optimism, resilience, creativity, and a touch of humor, you're well on your way to transforming your entrepreneurial dreams into reality. So, put on those entrepreneurial glasses, spot those opportunities, and let your passion drive you to success!

Facing Your Fears

Starting a business can be like standing on the edge of a diving board, peering into the deep, blue unknown. It's thrilling but also terrifying. Fear and doubt are natural companions on the entrepreneurial journey. The trick is not to let them drive the car. As Franklin D. Roosevelt famously said, "The only thing we have to fear is fear itself" (Roosevelt, F.D.).

Entrepreneurs often have to dive headfirst into uncertainty. Picture yourself as a superhero – let's call you Fear Crusher. Every time fear rears its ugly head, you give it a whack with your mighty hammer of confidence. It's okay to be scared; what's important is to keep moving forward despite the fear.

Strategies to Overcome Fear and Doubt

- Break It Down: Divide your big, scary goals into smaller, manageable tasks. It's easier to fight one tiny monster at a time than a giant dragon.

- Positive Visualization: Imagine the best possible outcomes instead of the worst. Visualizing success can be a powerful motivator.

- Action Over Perfection: Don't wait for the perfect moment to act. Remember, "Done is better than perfect" (Sheryl Sandberg).

Think of fear as that overly cautious friend who always says, "Are you sure that's a good idea?" before you try anything fun. Politely thank your friend for their concern, and then go ahead and do it anyway. You'll have a great story to tell, and who knows – you might just succeed.

Finding Your Yoda

In the epic journey of entrepreneurship, mentors and role models are like Yoda to your Luke Skywalker. They guide, support, and occasionally whack you with a stick when you're about to make a foolish decision. A good mentor can make all the difference, offering wisdom from their own experiences and helping you avoid common pitfalls.

The Importance of Mentorship

1. Experience Sharing: Mentors have been there, done that, and have the scars to prove it. They can share invaluable lessons learned from their successes and failures.

2. Networking: A mentor can open doors to new opportunities and connections. It's not just what you know but who you know.

3. Emotional Support: Entrepreneurship can be a lonely journey. Having someone to talk to who understands your struggles can be incredibly reassuring.

Choosing the Right Mentor

Look for someone who inspires you, who has achieved what you aspire to, and who genuinely wants to help you succeed. As Oprah Winfrey said, "A mentor is someone who allows you to see the hope inside yourself" (Winfrey, O.).

Dream Big

Building a vision for your start-up is like painting a masterpiece. It's about dreaming big but also about making those dreams tangible. Your vision is the North Star that will guide your business decisions and keep you focused.

Crafting Your Vision

1. Be Clear and Specific: Vague visions are like trying to navigate with a foggy windshield. Clearly define what success looks like for your start-up.

2. Inspire and Motivate: Your vision should excite you and your team. It's the why behind what you do. As Simon Sinek says, "People don't buy what you do; they buy why you do it" (Sinek, S.).

3. Be Flexible: While it's important to have a vision, it's also crucial to adapt as circumstances change. Think of your vision as a lighthouse guiding you, but be prepared to navigate around unexpected obstacles.

Imagine you're Steve Jobs, envisioning a world where everyone has a personal computer. At the time, it sounded like science fiction, but his clear and compelling vision drove Apple to create groundbreaking products that changed the world. Jobs famously said, "The people who are crazy enough to think they can change the world are the ones who do" (Jobs, S.).

The Journey Begins

Taking the first steps in your entrepreneurial journey can feel daunting. But remember, every marathon starts with a single step. You don't need to have everything figured out right away; you just need to start.

Key Initial Steps

1. Research and Validate: Make sure there's a market for your idea. Talk to potential customers, research competitors, and validate your assumptions.

2. Create a Business Plan: Outline your business model, target market, value proposition, and financial projections. Think of it as a roadmap for your journey.

3. Build a Minimum Viable Product (MVP): Start with a simple version of your product or service to test your idea and gather feedback. As Reid Hoffman said, "If you are not embarrassed by the first version of your product, you've launched too late" (Hoffman, R.).

4. Network: Connect with other entrepreneurs, potential mentors, and industry experts. Networking can open doors and provide valuable insights.

Imagine your start-up journey as a dance. You might feel like you have 2 left feet at first, but with each step, you'll gain confidence and rhythm. And hey, if you stumble, just laugh it off and keep dancing.

Entrepreneurship is all about enjoying the journey as much as the destination.

Overcoming fear and doubt, finding the right mentors, building a compelling vision, and taking those first crucial steps are all part of the entrepreneurial adventure. Embrace the process with humor, resilience, and passion. Remember, every successful entrepreneur started exactly where you are now – with a dream, a bit of courage, and the determination to turn their vision into reality. So go on, take that leap, and let the journey from start-up to success begin!

So, here's to all the dreamers, the risk-takers, and the innovators – may your entrepreneurial spark light up the world!

CHAPTER

II

TURNING IDEAS INTO REALITY

From Concept to Execution

Bridging the Gap: So, you've had your eureka moment, and your idea is fresh and exciting. Now what? Turning that shiny concept into a real, functioning business can feel like trying to turn a cat into a dog. It's a process that requires patience, perseverance, and a healthy dose of humor.

Picture this: You're standing on the edge of a cliff, your great idea strapped to your back like a parachute. Taking that first leap into execution is terrifying, but as Walt Disney wisely said, "The way to get started is to quit talking and begin doing" (Disney, W.).

Start small, test the waters, and don't be afraid to make mistakes. Remember, even if you belly flop, you're still in the water. Learn from your splash, adjust, and dive again.

Steps to Execution

1. Plan: Outline the steps needed to bring your idea to life. A good plan is like a GPS for your business journey.

2. Prototype: Create a basic version of your product. It doesn't have to be perfect – think of it as the IKEA furniture of your start-up, a little wobbly but functional.

3. Feedback: Get opinions from potential users. This is like having your friends over to help you figure out which part of the IKEA instruction manual you're holding upside down.

4. Refine: Use the feedback to make improvements. Each tweak gets you closer to that picture-perfect product.

Imagine Jeff Bezos starting Amazon in his garage. His first office was cramped, and the desk was made from a door – yes, a door! Bezos didn't let the humble beginnings stop him; he focused on execution. Today, Amazon is a behemoth. So, remember, you don't need a fancy start – you need a determined one.

Understanding Your Target Market

Market research is like going on a first date with your business idea and the market. You need to ask the right questions, listen carefully, and understand what the market likes and dislikes. It's all about finding the perfect match.

Why Market Research?

Skipping market research is like going to a party without knowing if it's a costume party or a black-tie event. You risk being the odd one out. As Henry Ford said, "If I had asked people what they wanted, they would have said faster horses" (Ford, H.). Ford knew that understanding the underlying needs of his customers was crucial, not just their immediate desires.

Techniques for Market Research

1. Surveys and Questionnaires: Think of these as speed dating sessions with potential customers. Quick and informative, and you'll know if there's potential for a second date.

2. Focus Groups: Gather a small group and dive deep into their preferences and pain points. It's like group therapy for your business idea.

3. Competitor Analysis: Stalk your competition like a detective on a TV drama. What are they doing right? Where are they missing the mark?

4. Social Media Listening: Eavesdrop on conversations in the digital world. What are people saying about your industry? Twitter and Instagram are the modern-day gossip corners.

Imagine launching a product without market research. It's like opening a taco stand in Italy – sure, some people might love it, but you're probably missing your main audience. Market research ensures you're selling tacos to taco lovers, not to a crowd expecting spaghetti.

Validating Your Idea

The proof is in the pudding: Validation is like taking your idea out for a test drive before committing to the long haul. It's about ensuring there's a real demand for what you're offering and that you're not just passionately pursuing a dead end.

Methods for Validation

1. Landing Pages: Create a simple website to gauge interest. Measure clicks and sign-ups to see if people are intrigued.

2. Crowdfunding: Platforms like Kickstarter can be great for testing the waters. If people are willing to fund your idea, you're onto something.

3. Pre-Sales: Sell your product before it's fully developed. If people are willing to pay in advance, it's a good sign.

4. Prototype Feedback: Share a prototype with a select group of potential customers and get their input. It's like letting people taste the cake batter before you bake the whole cake.

Think of Dropbox. Before writing a single line of code, the founders created a simple video explaining their concept. The overwhelmingly positive response validated their idea and attracted the first users and investors. As Dropbox founder Drew Houston said, "Don't worry about failure; you only have to be right once" (Houston, D.).

Validating your idea without proper feedback is like asking your mum if your stand-up comedy routine is funny. She'll laugh, but she's biased. Get out there and find your true audience – they'll tell you if your jokes (or product) really land.

Turning ideas into reality involves a blend of careful planning, thorough research, and brave execution. By bridging the gap between concept and action, understanding your market, and validating your idea, you lay a solid foundation for success. Remember, even the greatest entrepreneurs started somewhere, usually with a lot of uncertainty and a few good laughs along the way. So, gear up, take the leap, and let the journey from concept to execution begin!

Creating a Business Plan

Creating a business plan is like drafting the blueprint for a house. Without it, you might end up with a roof on the floor and a door in the ceiling. Your business plan is your roadmap, guiding you through the twists and turns of entrepreneurship.

Essential Components of a Business Plan

1. Executive Summary: Think of this as the "elevator pitch" of your business. If you can't explain your business in a few sentences, you might be too complicated. As Albert Einstein said, "If you can't explain it simply, you don't understand it well enough" (Einstein, A.).

Business Description: Describe what your business does, who your customers are, and why it matters. Imagine you're telling your grandma about it – simple, clear, and with a touch of excitement.

Market Analysis: Dive into your industry, market size, and competitors. It's like being a detective – the more you know, the better prepared you are.

Organization and Management: Outline your business's structure and team. Who's the boss? Who's the right-hand man? And most importantly, who brings the donuts?

Products or Services: Describe what you're selling. If you can make someone as excited about it as you are, you're on the right track.

Marketing and Sales Strategy: How will you attract and keep customers? It's like planning a party – you need to get people to come and then make sure they have a great time.

Funding Request: If you're seeking funding, explain how much you need and what you'll use it for. Be as clear and precise as if you're asking your friend for money and promising to return it (with interest!).

Financial Projections: Forecast your revenue, expenses, and profits. It's like peering into a crystal ball but with spreadsheets instead of mystic visions.

Imagine a business plan for a company that makes edible phone cases. The executive summary might read: "We're revolutionizing the tech industry with snackable phone cases – because sometimes you need to nibble while you talk!" It's quirky, but it gets the point across.

Building a Minimum Viable Product (MVP)

The Bare Necessities: Creating an MVP is like making a sandwich with just bread and butter before deciding to add the ham, cheese, and all the extras. It's about delivering the core functionality to test and learn from your users.

Steps to Create an MVP

Identify the Core Problem: What problem are you solving? Focus on the core issue, not the extra bells and whistles. As Steve Jobs said, "Deciding what not to do is as important as deciding what to do" (Jobs, S.).

1. Define the Essential Features: Strip your idea down to its most essential elements. Imagine your product as a pizza – start with the basic cheese before adding the fancy toppings.

2. Build the Simplest Version: Create a version of your product that does just enough to solve the problem. It's like a sketch before the full painting – simple but effective.

3. Launch Quickly: Get your MVP out to users as soon as possible. As Reid Hoffman said, "If you are not embarrassed by the first version of your product, you've launched too late" (Hoffman, R.).

4. Gather Feedback: Use user feedback to refine and improve your product. It's like getting taste testers for your new recipe – their insights are invaluable.

Think of an MVP for a self-watering plant pot. The MVP might just be a pot with a basic water reservoir and a simple mechanism to release water. Your pitch could be: "Introducing the Lazy Gardener's Dream – because even plants need a drink now and then!"

Prototyping and Product Development

Bringing Your Idea to Life: Prototyping is the process of creating a preliminary model of your product. It's like the dress rehearsal before the big show – essential for working out the kinks.

Steps in Prototyping

1. Conceptual Design: Sketch out your idea. This is your chance to play artist – get creative and think about how your product will look and feel.

2. Create a Physical Model: Use materials like cardboard, clay, or 3D printing to create a tangible version. It doesn't have to be perfect, just functional.

3. Test and Iterate: Put your prototype to the test. Gather feedback, make adjustments, and repeat. It's like baking cookies – taste-test, tweak the recipe, and bake again.

4. Refine the Design: Use the insights from testing to refine and perfect your product. Each iteration brings you closer to the final masterpiece.

Developing the Final Product

Once you have a working prototype, it's time to develop the final product. This involves fine-tuning the design, ensuring quality, and preparing for production.

1. Detail Design: Flesh out the finer details of your product. Think of it as adding the final touches to a painting – every stroke counts.

2. Pilot Production: Produce a small batch to test the manufacturing process. It's like making a few dozen cookies before committing to baking a thousand.

3. Quality Control: Ensure your product meets all quality standards. No one wants a cookie that crumbles at the first bite!

As Thomas Edison said, "Genius is one percent inspiration and ninety-nine percent perspiration" (Edison, T.). Prototyping and product development are where ninety-nine percent of hard work happens.

Creating a business plan, building an MVP, and developing prototypes are crucial steps in turning your idea into reality. Approach each step with a mix of seriousness and humor, and remember, even the most successful entrepreneurs started with a simple idea and a lot of determination. So, roll up your sleeves, embrace the journey, and get ready to bring your vision to life – one step (and one laugh) at a time.

Assembling Your Dream Team

Finding Your Avengers: Building your dream team is like assembling the Avengers. You need a diverse group of people with unique skills, all working together toward a common goal. As Steve Jobs famously said, "Great things in business are never done by one person; they're done by a team of people" (Jobs, S.).

Key Roles to Fill

1. The Visionary: The person with the big ideas. They see the future and steer the ship. Think of them as your Captain America.

2. The Tech Guru: The brains behind the operation, turning ideas into reality with their technical expertise. This is your Iron Man.

3. The Marketing Maven: They know how to get your message out there and attract customers. Your business's Black Widow.

4. The Operations Wizard: The person who ensures everything runs smoothly. Your Hawkeye is hitting all the operational targets.

5. The Financial Whiz: The one who keeps the books balanced and the cash flowing. Your Thor, hammering out the numbers.

Strategies for Recruitment

1. Network Like a Pro: Attend industry events, join online forums, and use LinkedIn to find potential team members. Remember, "Your network is your net worth" (Porter Gale).

2. Look for Passion: Skills can be taught, but passion is innate. Find people who believe in your vision as much as you do.

3. Cultural Fit: Ensure your team shares your values and work ethic. You want a team that's not just capable but also cohesive.

Imagine recruiting a team like a heist movie. You approach your tech guru and say, "We need someone who can hack into the mainframe." They respond, "I'm in. But only if we can use code names." Building a team should be fun, not just functional.

Funding Your Start-Up

The Quest for Cash: Securing funding for your start-up is like going on a treasure hunt. The treasure? Enough money to get your dream off the ground. Remember what Richard Branson said, "Business opportunities are like buses; there's always another one coming" (Branson, R.).

Overview of Funding Options

1. Bootstrapping: Using your own savings. It's the DIY approach – effective but can be risky.

2. Friends and Family: Borrowing from those close to you. Just be prepared for awkward Thanksgiving dinners if things go south.

3. Angel Investors: Wealthy individuals who invest in start-ups. Think of them as your business's fairy godparents.

4. Venture Capital: Firms that invest in high-growth potential companies. They're looking for the next unicorn.

5. Crowdfunding: Platforms like Kickstarter or Indiegogo. Let the public decide if your idea is worth funding.

Tips for Pitching to Investors

1. Tell a Compelling Story: Investors need to believe in you as much as your idea. Start with why you're passionate about your business.

2. Show the Numbers: Be prepared with solid financial projections. Investors love seeing potential ROI.

3. Be Prepared for Questions: Anticipate tough questions and practice your answers. Think of it as preparing for a job interview – for your dream job.

Imagine pitching your idea to a panel of investors. You start with, "So, what if I told you that you could invest in a company that's going to be bigger than Google and Apple combined? Just kidding, but seriously, here's why we're amazing..."

Branding and Positioning

Crafting Your Identity: Branding is more than just a logo or a catchy slogan. It's the essence of who you are as a company. Jeff Bezos said it best, "Your brand is what other people say about you when you're not in the room" (Bezos, J.).

Steps to Build a Strong Brand

1. Define Your Mission and Vision: What are your core values? What do you stand for? This is the heart of your brand.

2. Know Your Audience: Understand who your customers are and what they care about. Tailor your brand message to resonate with them.

3. Create a Visual Identity: Design a logo, choose your colors, and create a visual style. Consistency is key – you want people to recognize your brand instantly.

4. Develop Your Voice: How do you communicate with your audience? Are you formal, casual, or humorous? Find a voice that aligns with your brand identity.

Positioning Your Brand

1. Identify Your Unique Selling Proposition (USP): What makes you different from the competition? Highlight this in all your branding efforts.

2. Tell Your Story: Share the journey of your brand. People love a good story, especially if it involves overcoming challenges and achieving success.

3. Engage with Your Audience: Use social media, blogs, and other platforms to interact with your customers. Make them feel like they're part of your brand's journey.

A Fun Example: Imagine branding a company that makes quirky office supplies. Your tagline could be, "Making your 9-to-5 less mundane, one paperclip at a time." Your social media could feature playful posts like, "Our staplers don't just staple – they hug your papers together."

As Marty Neumeier said, "A brand is not what you say it is. It's what they say it is" (Neumeier, M.). Your job is to shape and guide that perception.

Assembling your dream team, securing funding, and building a strong brand are crucial steps in turning your start-up idea into a successful business. Approach each step with a mix of seriousness and humor. Remember, every successful entrepreneur started somewhere, usually with a lot of uncertainty and a few good laughs along the way. So, gear up, take the leap, and let the journey from start-up to success begin – one step (and one joke) at a time.

Marketing and Sales Strategy

Art of Attraction: Marketing and sales are like dating. You need to attract the right people, make a great first impression, and keep them interested for the long haul. Remember what Seth Godin said, "People do not buy goods and services. They buy relations, stories, and magic" (Godin, S.).

Developing an Effective Marketing Plan

1. Know Your Audience: Research who your customers are, what they need, and where they hang out. It's like knowing your crush's favorite coffee shop.

2. Create Compelling Content: Whether it's blog posts, videos, or social media updates, make your content engaging and valuable. Imagine telling a story so well that people forget to check their phones.

3. Leverage Social Media: Platforms like Instagram, Twitter, and LinkedIn are your stage. Use them to showcase your brand's personality and connect with your audience.

4. SEO and SEM: Make sure your website is optimized for search engines and consider investing in search engine marketing. It's like making sure you're always the top result when someone googles "best date ideas."

5. Email Marketing: Build an email list and send regular updates. It's like sending love letters to your customers – personal and thoughtful.

Sales Tactics to Attract and Retain Customers

1. Build Relationships: Sales is about building trust and relationships. Remember, people buy from people they like.

2. Listen More Than You Talk: Understand your customer's needs and tailor your pitch accordingly. It's like being a good conversationalist – listen first, speak second.

3. Follow-up: Persistence pays off. A polite follow-up can turn a maybe into a yes. Just don't be a stalker – there's a fine line!

Imagine your marketing campaign as a dating profile. "Hi, I'm Your Product. I enjoy solving your problems, making your life easier, and being there when you need me. Swipe right for success!"

Navigating Legal and Regulatory Hurdles

The Legal Jungle: Starting a business is exciting until you hit the jungle of legal and regulatory requirements. Think of it as an Indiana Jones adventure, complete with booby traps and hidden treasures. As Abraham Lincoln said, "A lawyer's time and advice are his stock in trade" (Lincoln, A.).

Understanding Legal Requirements

1. Business Structure: Decide whether you're a sole proprietorship, partnership, LLC, or corporation. Each has its own legal implications. It's like choosing your character in a video game – each comes with different powers and challenges.

2. Licenses and Permits: Make sure you have all the necessary licenses and permits to operate legally. This is your business's "permission to play."

3. Tax Obligations: Understand your tax obligations. No one likes taxes, but you don't want the IRS knocking on your door.

Protecting Your Intellectual Property

1. Trademarks: Register your brand name and logo to protect them. It's like putting a "Do Not Touch" sign on your most prized possessions.

2. Patents: If you have a unique product, consider patenting it. It's your way of saying, "Hands off, this is mine!"

3. Copyrights: Protect your original content. It's like a security system for your creative work.

Compliance with Regulations

1. Industry Regulations: Ensure you comply with regulations specific to your industry. It's like following the rules of a board game – break them, and you're out.

2. Employment Laws: Understand laws related to hiring, wages, and workplace safety. Treat your employees right, or you might end up with a mutiny on your hands.

3. Data Protection: Ensure you're compliant with data protection laws like GDPR. It's like being a bouncer at a club – only the right people get in.

Imagine navigating legal hurdles as a game of Monopoly. You've got to buy properties (register your business), avoid jail (comply with regulations), and hopefully, you don't end up broke from legal fees.

Building an Online Presence

Your Digital Footprint: In today's world, if you're not online, do you even exist? Building an online presence is like creating your digital persona – it's how the world sees you. As Bill Gates said, "If your business is not on the internet, then your business will be out of business" (Gates, B.).

Creating a Compelling Website

1. User-Friendly Design: Ensure your website is easy to navigate. Think of it as the layout of a well-organized house – everything in its place and easy to find.

2. Quality Content: Provide valuable content that answers your audience's questions. It's like being a helpful neighbor who always has the best advice.

3. Mobile Optimization: Make sure your site looks great on mobile devices. People use their phones more than they use their laptops.

Leveraging Social Media

1. Consistency: Post regularly and maintain a consistent brand voice. It's like being a reliable friend – always there when needed.

2. Engagement: Interact with your followers, respond to comments, and join conversations. Think of it as mingling at a party – be approachable and engaging.

3. Visual Appeal: Use high-quality images and videos. It's like dressing up for a first date – first impressions matter.

SEO Strategies

1. Keywords: Use relevant keywords to improve your search engine rankings. It's like giving your site a map to follow straight to the top of search results.

2. Backlinks: Get other reputable sites to link to yours. It's like having popular friends who vouch for you.

3. Content Updates: Regularly update your content to keep it fresh. Stale content is like old bread – nobody wants it.

A Fun Example: Imagine your online presence as a virtual storefront. Your website is the shop window, social media is the friendly greeter at the door, and SEO is the signpost directing people to your store.

Customer Acquisition and Retention

The Lifeblood of Your Business: Acquiring and retaining customers is like dating: you want to attract the right people, impress them, and keep them interested. As Peter Drucker said, "The purpose of business is to create and keep a customer" (Drucker, P.).

Strategies for Customer Acquisition

1. Know Your Target Audience: Identify your ideal customers. This is like choosing the right people to invite to your party—not everyone likes karaoke, but those who do will have a blast.

2. Offer Value: Ensure your product or service solves a problem or fulfills a need. Remember, "People don't buy products; they buy better versions of themselves" (Pabst, W.).

3. Leverage Digital Marketing: Use social media, email campaigns, and SEO to reach your audience. Think of it as casting a wide net to catch the right fish.

4. Referral Programs: Encourage your current customers to refer friends. It's like a "bring a friend" discount at your favorite restaurant.

Customer Retention Tactics

1. Excellent Customer Service: Be responsive, helpful, and friendly. It's like being the perfect host – making your guests feel special.

2. Loyalty Programs: Reward repeat customers. A coffee shop punch card may be old school, but it works!

3. Engage Regularly: Keep in touch through newsletters, social media, and personalized messages. It's like sending your grandma a card – she loves it!

4. Listen to Feedback: Act on customer suggestions and complaints. They'll appreciate it, and you'll improve. It's like letting someone else DJ for a while – you might discover great new music.

Imagine customer retention as keeping a goldfish alive. Feed them (value), clean their tank (customer service), and avoid overdoing it with fancy decorations (unnecessary features). Your goal is a happy, thriving goldfish—or customer.

Setting Up Operations

The Backbone of Your Business: Setting up operations is like organizing a concert. You need the right instruments, players, and a solid plan to pull off a great show. As Henry Ford said, "Coming together is a beginning; keeping together is progress; working together is success" (Ford, H.).

Key Aspects of Operations

Logistics and Supply Chain Management: Ensure you have reliable suppliers and efficient logistics. It's like ensuring your band's gear arrives at the venue on time.

1. Process Management: Develop efficient workflows and processes. Think of it as rehearsing until every note is perfect.

2. Technology and Tools: Invest in the right tools and software. It's like choosing the best guitar for your lead player.

3. Quality Control: Maintain high standards for your products or services. You don't want to hit a sour note!

Building a Strong Team

1. Hire Wisely: Choose skilled team members who fit your company culture. It's like casting the right actors for a play – everyone must play their part well.

2. Training and Development: Provide continuous learning opportunities. Think of it as band practice – the more you rehearse, the better you get.

3. Communication: Foster open and effective communication. It's like making sure everyone knows the setlist and timing.

Imagine setting up operations like preparing for a family road trip. You need to pack (logistics), plan the route (process management), ensure the car is in good shape (technology), and keep everyone entertained and happy (team management).

Measuring Success

Keeping Score: Measuring success is essential to understanding how well your business is doing. It's like checking the scoreboard during a game – you need to know if you're winning or need to up your game. As Peter Drucker wisely said, "What gets measured gets managed" (Drucker, P.).

Key Performance Indicators (KPIs)

1. Revenue and Profit Margins: Track your income and profitability. It's the ultimate measure of success – like the score in a basketball game.

2. Customer Acquisition Cost (CAC): Know how much it costs to acquire a new customer. It's like knowing how much you spend on snacks to lure people to your party.

3. Customer Lifetime Value (CLV): Estimate the total value a customer brings over their relationship with you. Think of it as the long-term value of a friendship.

4. Churn Rate: Measure how many customers leave over a period. It's like checking how many guests leave the party early – and figuring out why.

Tools for Measuring Success

1. Analytics Software: Use tools like Google Analytics, CRM systems, and financial software. They're your business's "Fitbit" – tracking everything you need to know.

2. Surveys and Feedback: Regularly gather customer feedback. It's like asking your friends how the party was – you'll know what to keep and change.

3. Regular Reviews: Set aside time to review your KPIs and make adjustments. Think of it as a performance review – but for your business.

Imagine measuring success like tracking your progress on a New Year's resolution. You start with high hopes (setting goals), track your progress (using KPIs), and occasionally adjust your expectations (because, let's face it, nobody's perfect).

Customer acquisition and retention, setting up operations, and measuring success are critical to building a thriving business. Approach each task with seriousness and humor, remembering that entrepreneurship is a journey of challenges and rewards. Keep your passion alive, laugh at the hiccups, and celebrate the victories – no matter how small. As you navigate this journey, remember that every great entrepreneur starts with a dream, a plan, and a lot of perseverance. So, take the leap, enjoy the ride, and watch your start-up become a success story!

Scaling Your Business

The Next Level: Scaling a business is like leveling up in a video game. You've conquered the initial challenges; now it's time to face bigger bosses and unlock new abilities. As Reid Hoffman put it, "First mover advantage doesn't go to the first company that launches; it goes to the first company that scales" (Hoffman, R.).

Strategies for Scaling

1. Build a Strong Foundation: Ensure your processes and systems can handle growth. It's like ensuring your castle has a solid foundation before adding more towers.

2. Automate and Delegate: Use technology to automate repetitive tasks and delegate responsibilities to your team. Remember, even Batman needs Alfred.

3. Expand Your Market: Target new markets or customer segments. It's like exploring new worlds in a game—there are always more treasures.

4. Focus on Quality: As you grow, maintain the quality of your product or service. Think of it as ensuring each new level in the game is just as engaging as the last.

Imagine scaling your business like inflating a balloon. You want it to grow bigger and bigger, but you need to ensure it doesn't pop. So, inflate carefully and keep an eye on any weak spots!

Overcoming Obstacles

The Hero's Journey: Every entrepreneur faces obstacles, but how you overcome them defines your success. As Thomas Edison said, "I have not failed. I've just found 10,000 ways that won't work" (Edison, T.).

Common Challenges and Solutions

1. Cash Flow Issues: Manage your finances carefully and look for ways to reduce costs. It's like being on a tight budget – sometimes, you must skip the fancy coffee.

2. Market Competition: Stay innovative and monitor your competitors. It's like a chess game—always think a few moves ahead.

3. Scaling Pains: Manage growth carefully to avoid overextending. It's like growing a plant – too much water, and it drowns; too little, and it withers.

4. Customer Retention: Keep your customers happy with excellent service and engagement. It's like hosting a party – ensure everyone's having a good time and wants to stay.

"Success is not final, failure is not fatal: It is the courage to continue that counts" (Churchill, W.). Embrace each challenge as an opportunity to learn and grow.

Imagine overcoming obstacles like navigating a maze. You'll hit dead ends, but with persistence and a bit of humor, you'll find your way out – and maybe discover some hidden cheese along the way!

Celebrating Milestones

Marking the Moments: Celebrating milestones is essential for motivation and morale. It's like reaching the checkpoint in a race – take a breather, enjoy the view, and gear up for the next leg. As Oprah Winfrey said, "The more you praise and celebrate your life, the more there is in life to celebrate" (Winfrey, O.).

Ways to Celebrate

1. Team Celebrations: Organize team events or parties. It's like throwing a mini-festival for your team – who doesn't love a good party?

2. Customer Appreciation: Offer special promotions or thank you notes to your customers. Think of it as giving your guests a party favor.

3. Personal Rewards: Treat yourself for reaching a milestone. You've earned it – maybe that fancy coffee, after all!

4. Public Recognition: Share your achievements on social media and with your community. It's like ringing the victory bell – let everyone hear it!

A Fun Example: Imagine celebrating milestones like winning a game show. Cue the confetti, music, and a big check (even if it's just symbolic). Make it fun and memorable!

Continuous Improvement

The Never-Ending Quest: Continuous improvement is the journey of striving to improve. It's like being on a quest in an RPG – there's always another level to achieve, another skill to master. As Tony Robbins said, "If you're not growing, you're dying" (Robbins, T.).

Strategies for Improvement

1. Regular Feedback: Collect and act on feedback from customers and employees. It's like getting a map with marked treasure spots – invaluable.

2. Stay Educated: Keep learning through courses, books, and industry news. Think of it as gathering new spells and abilities for your character.

3. Innovate: Always look for ways to improve your products or services. It's like updating your software – keep it current and efficient.

4. Set New Goals: Once you achieve a goal, set a new one. It's like finishing a quest and immediately picking up the next – the adventure continues.

"Without continual growth and progress, such words as improvement, achievement, and success have no meaning" (Franklin, B.). Keep moving forward, always striving for excellence.

Imagine continuous improvement, like trying to perfect your homemade pizza recipe. You'll have some cheesy disasters and doughy mishaps, but with each attempt, it gets more delicious. Just remember, even the mistakes are part of the fun!

Scaling your business, overcoming obstacles, celebrating milestones, and continuously improving are crucial elements of entrepreneurial success. Embrace each stage with determination, a bit of humor, and a willingness to learn. Remember, every great entrepreneur started with a dream and faced countless challenges along the way. Keep your passion alive, laugh at the bumps in the road, and celebrate every victory, big or small. Your journey from start-up to success is an adventure worth savoring, one step (and one joke) at a time.

CHAPTER

III

FINDING YOUR PASSION

The Importance of Passion in Entrepreneurship

Why Passion Matters: Passion is the secret sauce of entrepreneurship. It's what keeps you going when the going gets tough and makes your work feel like play. As Steve Jobs famously said, "The only way to do great work is to love what you do" (Jobs, S.).

1. Fueling Your Drive: Imagine running a marathon. Without passion, you'd be the person gasping for air at the first-mile marker, desperately searching for a cab. You're sprinting across the finish line with passion, arms raised in triumph, maybe even doing a victory dance. Passion gives you the stamina to endure the long haul of building a business.

2. A Personal Touch: Think about the times you've been so engrossed in an activity that you lost track of time. That's the power of passion. It transforms work from a chore into something you genuinely enjoy. Passionate entrepreneurs don't count hours; they make hours count.

Picture passion as your business's caffeine. Without it, you're a groggy mess struggling to keep your eyes open. With it, you're a hyper-focused machine ready to conquer the world. Don't overdo it; you might become jittery and incoherent – balance is key!

Self-Discovery and Identifying Your Passions

The Journey Within: Self-discovery is like being an archaeologist, but instead of digging for ancient artifacts, you uncover the layers of your interests and desires. Socrates was onto something when he said, "Know thyself" (Socrates).

Techniques for Self-Reflection

1. Mindfulness and Meditation: Take time to quiet your mind and listen to your inner voice. It's like tuning into a radio station playing your favorite songs.

2. Journaling: Write down your thoughts, dreams, and experiences. It's like conversing with yourself – just less weird than talking to a mirror.

3. Exploring Interests: Try new activities, read diverse books, and meet different people. It's like speed dating for hobbies – you never know which one might be the one.

Consider the tale of Joe, who spent years in a corporate job he hated. One day, while attending a friend's pottery class (under duress), he discovered a hidden talent for creating beautiful vases. Fast forward, and Joe now runs a successful pottery business. His secret? A little clay and a lot of passion.

Aligning Passion with Purpose

The Power Couple - Passion and Purpose: Passion and purpose are like peanut butter and jelly – they're great on their own, but together, they create something magical. As Simon Sinek said, "Working hard for something we don't care about is called stress; working hard for something we love is called passion" (Sinek, S.).

Finding Your Purpose

1. Identify Your Values: What principles guide your life? Your values are the compass that points toward your purpose.

2. Evaluate Your Impact: Consider how your passion can positively affect others. It's like using your superpower for the greater good.

3. Set Clear Goals: Align your passion with achievable goals that reflect your purpose. It's like setting a GPS route – you need a destination to start the journey.

Imagine aligning passion with purpose as finding the perfect dance partner. You can dance alone, but with the right partner, every step becomes more graceful and every move more meaningful. Just ensure your partner isn't stepping on your toes – that's a sign you must recalibrate!

Finding your passion is the cornerstone of entrepreneurial success. It fuels your drive, transforms work into joy, and helps you navigate the inevitable challenges. Self-discovery is the process of digging deep to uncover what truly excites you while aligning that passion with purpose ensures your efforts are meaningful and impactful. Embrace this journey with humor, reflection, and a sense of adventure. Remember, passion is not just about what you do but why you do it – which makes all the difference.

The Role of Curiosity and Exploration

Curiosity—The Entrepreneur's Best Friend: Curiosity is what a magnifying glass is to an entrepreneur and Sherlock Holmes—it reveals hidden clues and leads to exciting discoveries. Albert Einstein once said, "I have no special talent. I am only passionately curious" (Einstein, A.).

Embracing the Unknown

1. Ask Questions: Don't be afraid to question everything. Why do things work the way they do? How can they be improved? It's like being a toddler again – everything is new and fascinating.

2. Seek New Experiences: Try new things out of your comfort zone. Attend workshops, travel, and meet new people. It's like a treasure hunt – you never know what gems you'll find.

3. Stay Open-Minded: Be willing to learn and adapt. It's like having a Swiss Army knife – the more tools you have, the better equipped you are to handle any situation.

Imagine a cat (we'll call her Whiskers) who is endlessly curious about the world outside her cozy home. One day, she ventures into the garden, only to get startled by a garden gnome. After her initial shock, she realizes the garden is a playground full of adventures. Like Whiskers, your curiosity might lead you to unexpected (and initially intimidating) opportunities.

Turning Hobbies into Business Ideas

The Hobby-Entrepreneur Conversion: Turning a hobby into a business is like transforming your favorite pastime into a money-making machine. As Walt Disney said, "We keep moving forward, opening new doors, and doing new things because we're curious, and curiosity keeps leading us down new paths" (Disney, W.).

Steps to Turn Hobbies into Business Ideas

1. Identify Market Needs: Check if there's a demand for your hobby. It's like baking cookies – you want to ensure people crave your particular flavor.

2. Evaluate Your Skills: Assess if your hobby skills are strong enough to go pro. Think of it as turning from a home cook into a celebrity chef.

3. Start Small: Test the waters with a side hustle before diving full-time. It's like dipping your toes in the pool before committing to a swim.

4. Gather Feedback: Get opinions from potential customers and refine your offerings. It's like having your friends taste-test your new cookie recipe – their feedback is invaluable.

Imagine your hobby as a beloved pet. You wouldn't expect your cat to suddenly start earning her keep (unless you've trained her to perform in commercials). Similarly, turning a hobby into a business requires time, patience, and a lot of love.

Passion vs. Practicality: Finding the Balance

Walking the Tightrope: Balancing passion and practicality is like walking a tightrope – lean too far in one direction, and you'll fall. Mark Cuban wisely said, "Follow your passion… but first, make sure it's not a one-way ticket to being broke" (Cuban, M.).

Finding the Balance

1. Assess Viability: Ensure your passion has market potential. It's like making sure your favorite dessert is tasty not just to you but also to others.

2. Create a Plan: Develop a solid business plan that includes practical steps to achieve your goals. Think of it as mapping out a road trip – you need a route, gas stations, and maybe a few snack stops.

3. Stay Flexible: Be willing to adapt and pivot if necessary. It's like dancing – sometimes you lead, sometimes you follow, but you always keep moving.

Imagine balancing passion and practicality like making a sandwich. Passion is the delicious filling, and practicality is the bread that holds it all together. Without the bread, you'd just have a mess; without the filling, it's just plain bread – not very exciting!

Curiosity and exploration are essential in uncovering new opportunities and fueling innovation. Turning hobbies into business ideas can transform your passion into a fulfilling career, but it requires careful consideration and testing. Balancing passion with practicality ensures that your business is both enjoyable and viable. Embrace these aspects with humor and a sense of adventure, and you'll be well on your way to entrepreneurial success. Remember, it's the curious mind that discovers new paths, the passionate heart that pursues them, and the practical plan that ensures they're sustainable.

Overcoming Fear and Doubt in Pursuing Passion

Embracing the Fear Factor: Fear and doubt are like uninvited guests at the party of entrepreneurship. They show up, eat all your snacks, and leave you questioning your life choices. But as Nelson Mandela said, "I learned that courage was not the absence of fear, but the triumph over it" (Mandela, N.).

Strategies to Overcome Fear and Doubt

1. Face Your Fears: Identify what scares you about pursuing your passion. It's like shining a flashlight in a dark room – things are less scary when you can see them clearly.

2. Take Small Steps: Break down your goals into manageable tasks. Imagine you're climbing a mountain. Don't focus on the peak; focus on the next step.

3. Seek Support: Surround yourself with supportive people who believe in you. Think of them as your cheerleaders, always ready to give you a motivational pep talk.

4. Practice Self-Compassion: Be kind to yourself. Remember, even superheroes have off days – Batman didn't catch the Joker every time.

Picture fear as a grumpy cat sitting on your keyboard while you're trying to work. It's annoying and persistent, but with a bit of patience (and maybe some treats), you can coax it away. Plus, once you've dealt with the cat, everything else seems easy in comparison!

Passion as a Long-Term Commitment

The Marathon, Not a Sprint: Passion isn't just a spark; it's a steady flame that needs tending. As Tony Robbins put it, "People are not lazy. They simply have impotent goals – that is, goals that do not inspire them" (Robbins, T.). Your passion is what keeps the flame burning, even when the winds of challenge blow strong.

Maintaining Long-Term Commitment

1. Set Realistic Goals: Create achievable milestones to keep you motivated. It's like playing a video game – you need those checkpoints to keep going.

2. Stay Adaptable: Be open to change and willing to pivot if necessary. Think of your passion as a river – sometimes, you need to follow its twists and turns.

3. Keep Learning: Continuously improve your skills and knowledge. Imagine you're a wizard at Hogwarts – there's always a new spell to learn or a potion to brew.

4. Celebrate Small Wins: Acknowledge and celebrate every little success. It's like rewarding yourself with a piece of chocolate every time you finish a chapter of a book – sweet and motivating.

Consider passion as a long-term relationship. It has its honeymoon phase, but it also requires work, patience, and the occasional romantic gesture (like buying yourself a new gadget or taking a mental health day). And just like any relationship, communication (with yourself) is key!

The Intersection of Skills and Passion

Finding Your Sweet Spot: The intersection of skills and passion is like the perfect recipe – when combined, they create something extraordinary. As Confucius said, "Choose a job you love, and you will never have to work a day in your life" (Confucius).

Identifying Your Skills

- Self-Assessment: Take stock of your skills and talents. It's like making an inventory of your superhero powers – know what you're capable of.

- Seek Feedback: Ask friends, colleagues, or mentors for their perspective on your strengths. Think of them as your personal mirrors – reflecting your best traits.

- Explore Training: Enroll in courses or workshops to enhance your skills. Imagine it's like leveling up in a role-playing game – every new skill makes you stronger.

Combining Skills and Passion

1. Find the Overlap: Look for areas where your skills and passions intersect. It's like finding the perfect Venn diagram – the sweet spot is where magic happens.

2. Experiment: Try different approaches to see what works best. It's like cooking – sometimes you need to tweak the recipe to get it just right.

3. Stay Committed: Work consistently to develop your skills in line with your passion. Think of it as tending a garden – regular care yields the best fruits.

Imagine your skills and passion as 2 best friends trying to start a band. Your skills playing the instruments and your passion sings the lead vocals. Together, they create harmonious (and sometimes hilariously off-key) music. Just make sure they don't start arguing over who gets to be the frontman!

Overcoming fear and doubt, committing to your passion for the long-term, and finding the intersection of your skills and passion are crucial steps in the entrepreneurial journey. Embrace fear as a part of the process, nurture your passion with dedication, and combine your skills to create something unique. Remember, the path to success is filled with challenges, but with a bit of humor, patience, and a lot of passion, you can turn your dreams into reality. As you navigate this journey, keep in mind that every great entrepreneur started somewhere – and so can you.

Inspiration from Successful Entrepreneurs

Learning from the Greats: Every successful entrepreneur has a story that can inspire and guide you on your journey. As Steve Jobs famously said, "Your work is going to fill a large part of your life, and the only way to be truly satisfied is to do what you believe is great work" (Jobs, S.).

Real-Life Stories

1. Steve Jobs (Apple): Jobs' journey was filled with ups and downs, from being ousted from Apple to returning and transforming it into one of the most valuable companies in the world. His story teaches us the importance of resilience and innovation.

2. Sara Blakely (Spanx): Starting with just $5,000 in savings, Blakely built a billion-dollar empire by revolutionizing women's undergarments. She faced countless rejections but persevered with humor and determination. She once joked, "Failure is not the outcome – failure is not trying" (Blakely, S.).

3. Elon Musk (Tesla, SpaceX): Musk's vision for the future has led to groundbreaking advancements in electric vehicles and space travel. He's faced numerous setbacks, including near bankruptcy, but his relentless pursuit of his passions has changed the world. Musk once quipped, "When something is important enough, you do it even if the odds are not in your favor" (Musk, E.).

Imagine if these entrepreneurs had given up early on. Jobs would be a Zen monk, Blakely would still be selling fax machines, and Musk might be an eccentric science teacher. Their stories remind us that success often comes from persevering through the most challenging times.

The Role of Mentors in Finding Your Passion

Mentorship - The Secret Sauce: Mentors are like the GPS for your entrepreneurial journey – they help you navigate the tricky terrain and avoid dead ends. Oprah Winfrey once said, "A mentor is someone who allows you to see the hope inside yourself" (Winfrey, O.).

Finding the Right Mentor

1. Look for Experience: Seek mentors who have walked the path you're on. It's like having a tour guide who's been to the hidden gems you're eager to discover.

2. Seek Compatibility: Choose someone whose values and vision align with yours. Imagine trying to duet with someone who's tone-deaf – it's just not going to work.

3. Ask Questions: Don't be afraid to reach out and ask for guidance. Remember, even Yoda needed Luke to ask for help.

Benefits of Mentorship

1. Guidance and Advice: Mentors provide invaluable insights and advice. Think of them as your personal business consultants – minus the hefty fee.

2. Support and Encouragement: They cheer you on and boost your confidence. Imagine having your own personal cheerleader who's been to the Super Bowl.

3. Networking Opportunities: Mentors often introduce you to valuable connections. It's like getting VIP access to the best business parties.

Consider a young entrepreneur, Tim, who had a brilliant idea for a new app but no clue how to start. Enter his mentor, Jane, a seasoned entrepreneur. Jane's first piece of advice? "Tim, unless your app can walk dogs or cook dinner, you might need to tweak it." They both laughed, and Tim realized the importance of honest, experienced feedback.

Creating a Vision Board for Your Passion

Visualizing Your Success: A vision board is like a map of your dreams, guiding you toward your goals. It's a powerful tool that turns abstract ideas into tangible plans. As Walt Disney said, "If you can dream it, you can do it" (Disney, W.).

Steps to Create an Effective Vision Board

1. Gather Supplies: Get a board, magazines, scissors, glue, and markers. It's like arts and crafts time – but for adults with serious dreams.

2. Define Your Goals: Clearly outline your short-term and long-term goals. Think of it as plotting the key destinations on your entrepreneurial road trip.

3. Collect Images and Words: Find pictures and words that represent your goals and dreams. It's like creating a visual playlist of your favorite songs – each one resonates with a part of you.

4. Arrange and Assemble: Arrange your images and words on the board in a way that inspires you. Imagine you're Michelangelo, but instead of the Sistine Chapel, you're creating a masterpiece for your future.

Creating a vision board can be a bit like making a collage in kindergarten – except now, your glue-sticking skills have a higher purpose. And don't worry if your vision board looks like a mess to others; it only needs to make sense to you. Just don't accidentally use pictures of someone else's dreams – you might end up as a professional llama farmer.

Drawing inspiration from successful entrepreneurs, finding the right mentor, and creating a vision board are essential steps in turning your passion into a thriving business. These tools help you overcome obstacles, stay focused, and maintain a clear vision of your goals. Embrace these strategies with humor and creativity, and remember that every great entrepreneur starts with a dream, a plan, and a bit of courage. Whether you're taking the first step or the hundredth, keep pushing forward with passion and persistence. Your success story is just beginning!

Testing and Validating Your Passion

Putting Your Passion to the Test: Testing your passion is like taking your favorite recipe and sharing it with friends – you need to see if others love it as much as you do. As Mark Twain said, "The secret of getting ahead is getting started" (Twain, M.).

Steps to Validate Your Passion

1. Market Research: Investigate if there's a demand for what you're passionate about. It's like figuring out if your gourmet avocado toast has a market beyond your kitchen.

2. Prototyping: Create a basic version of your product or service. Think of it as the beta version of your favorite video game – you need feedback before the big release.

3. Gather Feedback: Ask potential customers for their honest opinions. Picture this as your mom's friends taste-testing your new cookie recipe – they'll tell you if it needs more chocolate.

4. Iterate and Improve: Use the feedback to refine your offering. Imagine you're a sculptor, chiseling away until you reveal your masterpiece.

Testing your passion is like singing karaoke. You might think you sound like Beyoncé, but the real test is the audience's reaction. If they're covering their ears, you know it's time to adjust your pitch.

Building a Support Network

The Power of Community: Building a support network is crucial for any entrepreneur. As Helen Keller said, "Alone we can do so little; together we can do so much" (Keller, H.).

Ways to Build Your Support Network

1. Family and Friends: Start with the people who know and believe in you. They're your first cheerleaders and toughest critics (thanks, Mom!).

2. Mentors and Advisers: Seek out experienced individuals who can offer guidance and advice. Think of them as your business Yoda's – wise and always ready with a nugget of wisdom.

3. Networking Events: Attend industry conferences and meetups. It's like speed dating for professionals – you never know who might be a perfect match for your business needs.

4. Online Communities: Join forums and social media groups related to your field. These are your virtual coffee shops where you can discuss ideas and get feedback.

Imagine trying to assemble IKEA furniture without any help – frustrating, right? Now imagine doing it with friends. Sure, there might be a few extra screws at the end, but at least you had fun (and maybe created a new modern art piece in the process).

Staying Motivated and Avoiding Burnout

The Marathon of Motivation: Staying motivated over the long haul is like running a marathon. As Vince Lombardi said, "The man on top of the mountain didn't fall there" (Lombardi, V.). It takes persistence and determination.

Strategies to Stay Motivated

1. Set Clear Goals: Break down your big dreams into smaller, manageable tasks. It's like eating an elephant one bite at a time – not that you should eat an elephant!

2. Celebrate Small Wins: Acknowledge and reward yourself for each milestone. Think of it as giving yourself a high-five – it's uplifting and keeps you going.

3. Stay Balanced: Ensure you have a healthy work-life balance. Imagine you're a tightrope walker – you need both focus and balance to stay on the wire.

4. Seek Inspiration: Surround yourself with motivational quotes, books, and people. It's like having a playlist of your favorite pump-up songs – they keep you energized.

Avoiding Burnout

1. Take Breaks: Don't be afraid to step away and recharge. It's like hitting the refresh button on your browser – everything runs smoother afterward.

2. Practice Self-Care: Ensure you're eating well, exercising, and getting enough sleep. Think of your body as a car – it needs fuel and maintenance to run efficiently.

3. Delegate: Don't try to do everything yourself. Delegate tasks to others when possible. Remember, even superheroes have sidekicks.

Staying motivated and avoiding burnout is like maintaining a healthy relationship with coffee. Too little, and you're groggy; too much, and you're jittery and talking to your plants. Find the sweet spot that keeps you energized without sending you into overdrive.

Testing and validating your passion, building a strong support network, and staying motivated while avoiding burnout are essential steps for any entrepreneur. These strategies ensure that your passion is not only viable but also sustainable over the long haul. Embrace these steps with humor, patience, and a positive mindset, and remember that every successful entrepreneur has faced similar challenges. Keep pushing forward with resilience and determination, and your journey from start-up to success will be both fulfilling and rewarding.

IV

FUNDING AND FINANCIAL MANAGEMENT

Assessing Your Capital Requirements

Understanding your funding needs is like figuring out how many slices of pizza you'll need for a party. If there are too few, your guests will be left hungry (and possibly angry). Too many, and you'll be eating leftovers for a week. In business, knowing your financial requirements means identifying initial setup costs, ongoing operational expenses, and potential future investments.

Estimating Initial and Ongoing Expenses

1. Initial Costs: These include one-time expenses such as registration fees, legal costs, initial inventory, and equipment purchases. Picture this as the cost of buying all the ingredients and setting up your kitchen for that pizza party.

2. Operational Expenses: These are your recurring costs like rent, utilities, salaries, and marketing. Think of them as the ongoing cost of keeping your pizza oven running and your ingredients fresh.

Differentiating Between Fixed and Variable Costs

1. Fixed Costs: These are expenses that remain constant regardless of your business activity, such as rent and salaries. They're like your pizza oven – whether you bake one pizza or a hundred, the oven's cost doesn't change.

2. Variable Costs: These fluctuate with your level of production or sales, such as materials and shipping. Imagine the more pizzas you make, the more dough and toppings you'll need.

Understanding your funding needs is like trying to predict how much your dog will eat at a barbecue. Plan too little, and you'll have a hungry dog; plan too much, and you'll be out of ribs.

Bootstrapping: The Art of Self-Funding

Utilizing Personal Savings and Resources: Bootstrapping is the entrepreneurial equivalent of pulling yourself up by your bootstraps – it's all about self-reliance. You're not just the CEO; you're the CFO, the marketing department, and sometimes even the janitor. As Richard Branson said, "Business opportunities are like buses; there's always another one coming" (Branson, R.).

Managing Finances on a Shoestring Budget

1. Frugality: When bootstrapping, every dollar counts. You become a master of DIY and bargain hunting. It's like using coupons for everything – from your office supplies to your software subscriptions.

2. Resourcefulness: You find creative solutions to problems. Need a marketing campaign? Maybe it's time to become best friends with social media influencers or create viral content on TikTok.

Advantages and Challenges of Bootstrapping

Advantages:

1. Control: You retain full ownership and control over your business decisions.

2. Financial Discipline: You learn to manage money wisely from the get-go.

Challenges:

1. Limited Resources: Without external funding, scaling can be slow.

2. Personal Risk: You're investing your own money, which can be risky if things don't go as planned.

Bootstrapping is like camping in the wilderness. It's challenging and resource-intensive, and sometimes you wonder why you didn't just stay home. But when you finally start that campfire (or land your first big client), it's all worth it.

Friends and Family Funding

Approaching Loved Ones for Investment: Asking friends and family for funding can feel like asking them to support your passion for collecting antique toasters. It's personal and can be awkward, but if done right, it can provide the necessary funds without the red tape.

Setting Clear Terms and Expectations

1. Transparency: Be clear about how much you need, how it will be used, and the potential risks. This isn't just borrowing $20 for gas money; it's an investment.

2. Formal Agreements: Draft a simple contract outlining the terms, including repayment or equity stakes. Think of it as a friendship prenup – better safe than sorry.

Balancing Personal Relationships and Business

1. Communication: Regular updates and open communication are key. Keep them in the loop about the business progress and challenges.

2. Professionalism: Treat their investment with the same respect and seriousness as you would with any other investor. Remember, Uncle Bob's $5,000 is still $5,000, even if he gave it to you at the family BBQ.

Asking friends and family for money can be like borrowing their prized lawnmower. If you don't return it in top shape (or at all), Thanksgiving dinners might get a bit awkward.

"The secret of getting ahead is getting started." – Mark Twain

Understanding funding needs is like deciding how many pairs of shoes to bring on vacation. Too few, and you're in trouble; too many, and you're paying for extra baggage.

Angel Investors: The Early-Stage Boost

Identifying and Pitching to Angel Investors: Angel investors are like the fairy godparents of the start-up world. They come in, wave their magic wands (or, in this case, their checkbooks), and help your business dreams come true. But unlike fairy tales, securing an angel investor requires more than just a catchy pitch – you need a solid business plan and a compelling story.

The Benefits and Risks of Angel Investment

Benefits:

1. Experience and Mentorship: Angel investors often bring valuable expertise and industry connections. As one wise angel investor put it, "Invest in people, not just ideas" (Thiel, P.).

2. Flexibility: Angels tend to be more flexible with their investment terms compared to venture capitalists.

Risks:

1. Equity Dilution: You're giving up a piece of your company, which means less control over decisions.

2. Pressure to Perform: With an investor onboard, the stakes are higher, and expectations are clear.

Case Studies of Successful Angel-Funded Start-Ups

Take, for example, the story of Airbnb. In its early days, Airbnb struggled to get funding. It wasn't until angel investor Paul Graham saw the potential and offered guidance and funding that the company started to take off. Now, Airbnb is a household name, and it all began with an angel's boost.

Pitching to an angel investor can feel like a first date. You're nervous, trying to look your best, and hoping they fall in love with your idea. Just remember, even if they don't swipe right, there are plenty of other angels in the sky.

Venture Capital: Attracting Investors

Understanding Venture Capital and How It Works: Venture capitalists (VCs) are like the sharks in "Shark Tank," but without the dramatic music and TV cameras. They invest large sums of money in promising start-ups in exchange for equity, hoping for substantial returns. As Mark Cuban once said, "Sweat equity is the most valuable equity there is" (Cuban, M.).

Preparing a Compelling Pitch Deck

Your pitch deck is your storybook, and you are the storyteller. It should include:

1. Problem and Solution: Clearly define the problem your start-up solves and how.

2. Market Opportunity: Show the size and growth potential of your target market.

3. Business Model: Explain how you plan to make money.

4. Traction: Highlight any milestones or achievements to date.

5. Team: Showcase the strengths and experience of your team.

6. Financial Projections: Provide realistic and achievable financial forecasts.

Negotiating Terms and Valuations

Negotiating with VCs can feel like a high-stakes poker game. You need to know your worth and be prepared to walk away if the terms aren't favorable. Remember, giving away too much equity too early can haunt you later.

Imagine you're at a flea market, haggling over a vintage lamp. You know its worth, but the seller wants a fortune. The key is to find a middle ground where both parties feel they've won. That's exactly what negotiating with a VC is like, except the stakes are much higher than a quirky lamp.

Crowdfunding: Power to the People

Choosing the Right Crowdfunding Platform: Crowdfunding platforms like Kickstarter and Indiegogo are the town squares of the digital age, where you can pitch your idea to the masses. It's democracy in action – if people love your idea, they'll fund it.

Crafting a Successful Crowdfunding Campaign

1. Engaging Story: Your campaign needs a compelling narrative that resonates emotionally with potential backers.

2. Attractive Rewards: Offer enticing rewards that make people want to support you, from early access to your product to exclusive experiences.

3. Visual Appeal: High-quality photos and videos can significantly boost your campaign's appeal. Think of it as the trailer to your blockbuster movie.

Examples of Successful Crowdfunding Stories

One of the most famous crowdfunding success stories is that of the Pebble smartwatch. They aimed to raise $100,000 but ended up securing over $10 million from eager backers. Their secret? A compelling pitch, a great product, and rewards that people wanted.

Running a crowdfunding campaign is like throwing a party and hoping people show up. You've got to have great music (your pitch), tasty snacks (your rewards), and a lot of energy to keep everyone engaged. And just like a party, there's always that one friend who promises to come and never shows up.

"The best way to predict the future is to create it."

– Peter Drucker.

Remember, "Money can't buy happiness, but it can fund a start-up, which is pretty close!"

Grants and Competitions

Finding and Applying for Grants: Applying for grants is like searching for hidden treasure – it's out there, but you need a good map and a bit of patience. Grants are non-repayable funds provided by governments, organizations, or foundations to support business projects. The trick is finding the ones that align with your start-up's goals.

1. Research: Start by identifying grants that match your business sector and objectives. Websites like Grants.gov and Foundation Directory Online can be goldmines of information.

2. Application: Craft a compelling narrative that clearly outlines your project, its impact, and why it deserves funding. Pay attention to details and follow all guidelines meticulously.

Competing in Business Competitions

Business competitions are like "Shark Tank" without the TV cameras. They offer cash prizes, mentorship, and invaluable exposure.

1. Preparing Your Pitch: Your pitch should be clear, concise, and compelling. Highlight your unique value proposition, market potential, and the problem you're solving.

2. Showcasing Your Innovation: Judges love innovation. Show how your product or service is a game-changer in your industry.

Applying for a grant is like preparing for a marathon. You need to train (research), have a strategy (write a strong application), and keep your spirits high (maintain optimism). And just like a marathon, crossing the finish line (getting the grant) makes all the hard work worthwhile.

Imagine applying for grants as a kid, trying to convince their parents why they need a new toy. You present your case, highlight all the benefits, and maybe even throw in a few promises about better behavior. The stakes are high, and so is the anticipation.

Bank Loans and Lines of Credit

Understanding Different Types of Bank Loans: Bank loans are like ordering from a menu – there are several options, and each has its own flavor. From term loans to lines of credit, understanding the differences is crucial.

1. Term Loans: These are lump-sum loans paid back over a fixed period with interest. Ideal for significant one-time investments, like purchasing equipment.

2. Lines of Credit: These work like a credit card, offering you a maximum limit from which you can draw as needed and pay back with interest. Great for managing cash flow fluctuations.

Applying for a Business Loan

1. Prepare Your Documents: Banks love paperwork. Have your business plan, financial statements, tax returns, and collateral details ready.

2. Build a Relationship: Get to know your banker. Having a good rapport can sometimes make the difference between a yes and a no.

Taking out a bank loan can feel like dating. You dress up (prepare your documents), have a polite conversation (your application), and hope they call you back with good news. Just remember, not all dates (or loans) are a match made in heaven; most are in hell.

Financial Fundamentals

Managing Cash Flow: Cash flow is the lifeblood of your business. It's like your daily coffee – without it, things can quickly go downhill. Managing it effectively ensures you can cover your expenses and invest in growth opportunities.

1. Forecasting: Predict your inflows and outflows to avoid cash crunches. It's like planning your grocery shopping – knowing how much you need and when.

2. Monitoring: Regularly review your cash flow statements to stay on top of your financial health.

Budgeting for Growth

1. Budgeting is like dieting – it requires discipline and a clear plan. Allocate funds to various aspects of your business, prioritize essential expenditures, and cut down on unnecessary costs.

2. Fixed vs. Variable Costs: Understand what costs are consistent (fixed) and which ones fluctuate (variable).

3. Contingency Fund: Always have a buffer for unexpected expenses. It's your business's rainy-day fund.

Think of managing cash flow like trying to keep your New Year's resolutions. You start with great intentions (your budget), but life throws temptations your way (unexpected expenses). Staying disciplined is key to achieving your goals.

"A budget is telling your money where to go instead of wondering where it went."

– Dave Ramsey.

Cash Flow Management

The Lifeblood of Your Business: Cash flow is the unsung hero of your business operations. It's the money moving in and out of your company, and without proper management, even profitable businesses can run into trouble. As Warren Buffett wisely said, "Cash combined with courage in a time of crisis is priceless" (Buffett, W.).

Forecasting Cash Flow

Forecasting your cash flow is like trying to predict the weather in your hometown – necessary but occasionally unpredictable. Start by estimating your future income and expenses based on historical data. This will help you anticipate periods of surplus or shortage and plan accordingly.

1. Monthly Projections: Regularly update your cash flow projections to reflect actual performance and adjust for any changes in your business environment.

2. Monitoring Inflows and Outflows: Keep a close eye on when you expect to receive payments and when you need to make them. Avoid the dreaded cash flow crunch by timing your expenses to match your revenue.

Tips for Managing Cash Flow

1. Speed Up Receivables: Encourage faster payment by offering discounts for early payments or implementing stricter payment terms.

2. Delay Payables: Take advantage of supplier credit terms to keep cash in your business longer.

1. Maintain a Cash Reserve: Having a cash reserve is like carrying an umbrella – you might not need it every day, but you'll be glad you have it when it rains.

Managing cash flow can sometimes feel like juggling flaming torches – thrilling but risky. Just remember, unlike the circus, you can't afford to drop the ball (or the torch).

Budgeting for Growth

Creating a Realistic Budget: Budgeting for growth is like planning a road trip. You need to know your destination (growth goals), map out the route (strategies), and pack enough snacks (funds) for the journey.

1. Setting Clear Objectives: Define your growth goals. Are you looking to expand your product line, enter new markets, or increase your customer base?

2. Allocating Resources: Prioritize spending on activities that directly contribute to growth, such as marketing, R&D, and talent acquisition.

Monitoring and Adjusting Your Budget

1. Regular Reviews: Conduct monthly or quarterly reviews to compare your actual performance against your budget. Adjust your budget as needed to stay on track.

2. Flexibility: Be prepared to pivot and reallocate resources if unexpected opportunities or challenges arise.

Think of your budget as your business's diet plan. It's all about balancing what you consume (expenses) and what you burn off (revenue). Occasionally, you'll need to adjust for cheat days (unexpected costs), but overall, stick to the plan to see growth.

Profitability Analysis

Understanding Profit Margins: Profitability analysis is like checking the engine of your car – it ensures everything is running smoothly and efficiently. Profit margins, in particular, tell you how much money you're making after covering your costs.

1. Gross Profit Margin: This is your revenue minus the cost of goods sold (COGS). It shows how efficiently you're producing your products or services.

2. Net Profit Margin: This is your bottom line – revenue minus all expenses. It indicates the overall profitability of your business.

Key Performance Indicators (KPIs)

1. Return on Investment (ROI): Measures the profitability of your investments. It's like checking the fuel efficiency of your car – the higher, the better.

2. Break-Even Analysis: Determines the sales volume needed to cover all costs. Knowing your break-even point is crucial for making informed business decisions.

Tips for Improving Profitability

1. Cost Control: Regularly review your expenses and identify areas where you can cut costs without compromising quality.

2. Pricing Strategy: Ensure your prices reflect the value you provide and cover all your costs, including a reasonable profit margin.

3. Product Mix Optimization: Focus on selling higher-margin products or services to boost overall profitability.

Profitability analysis can sometimes feel like reading a complex recipe. There are a lot of ingredients (costs), and you need to mix them in the right proportions to get the desired result (profit). And just like cooking, sometimes it's okay to add a little extra spice (creativity) to enhance the flavor (profit).

"Accounting is the language of business."

– Warren Buffett.

Financial Planning for the Future

Setting Long-Term Financial Goals: Financial planning for the future is like preparing for a marathon – you need endurance, a strategy, and the occasional energy gel pack (savings). It's essential to set clear long-term goals that guide your business growth.

1. Vision and Mission: Define your business's vision and mission. These are the guiding stars that will help you navigate through financial decisions.

2. SMART Goals: Set Specific, Measurable, Achievable, Relevant, and Time-bound (SMART) financial goals. Whether it's doubling your revenue in 5 years or expanding to new markets, having clear targets will keep you focused.

Building a Financial Plan

1. Revenue Projections: Estimate your future revenue based on market trends and historical performance. Remember, optimism is great, but realism keeps you afloat.

2. Expense Management: Forecast your future expenses, considering both fixed and variable costs. Plan for potential increases in costs as your business scales.

Planning for Unexpected Events

1. Emergency Fund: Just like carrying an umbrella on a sunny day, an emergency fund prepares you for unexpected financial storms. Aim to set aside at least 6 months of operating expenses.

2. Insurance: Protect your business with appropriate insurance coverage, such as liability, property, and key person insurance.

Financial planning can feel like trying to predict the weather 6 months in advance. You pack your sunscreen and your snow boots, hoping you'll be ready for anything. Just remember, flexibility is key – and maybe keep an extra pair of socks handy.

Tax Planning and Compliance

Understanding Tax Obligations: Taxes are like the in-laws of business – inevitable and sometimes challenging to deal with, but they must be addressed. Knowing your tax obligations is crucial to avoid unpleasant surprises.

1. Business Structure: Your business structure (sole proprietorship, partnership, corporation) affects your tax obligations. Choose the structure that offers the best tax benefits.

2. Types of Taxes: Be aware of federal, state, and local taxes applicable to your business. This includes income tax, payroll tax, sales tax, and property tax.

Strategies for Tax Planning

1. Deductions and Credits: Maximize your deductions and credits to reduce your taxable income. Expenses like office supplies, travel, and marketing can often be deducted.

2. Timing Income and Expenses: Strategically time your income and expenses to manage your tax liability. For example, defer income to the next year if you anticipate being in a lower tax bracket.

Staying Compliant

1. Record Keeping: Maintain detailed and accurate records of all financial transactions. This makes tax time less stressful and helps in case of an audit.

2. Professional Help: Consider hiring a tax professional to navigate complex tax laws and ensure compliance.

Filing taxes can feel like preparing for a school exam you forgot to study for – you frantically gather all your notes (receipts) and hope you remember enough to pass (file correctly). And just like in school, it's always good to have a smart friend (tax adviser) to help out.

Hiring a Financial Adviser or Accountant

The Value of Professional Advice: Hiring a financial adviser or accountant is like having a seasoned travel guide on a journey to an unfamiliar destination. They know the shortcuts, the pitfalls, and the best places to invest your resources.

1. Expertise: Financial advisers provide investment advice, retirement planning, and wealth management services. Accountants handle bookkeeping, tax preparation, and financial reporting.

2. Peace of Mind: Professional help can reduce stress and free up your time to focus on growing your business.

Choosing the Right Professional

1. Credentials: Look for certified professionals (e.g., CPA for accountants, CFP for financial advisers). Certifications indicate a high level of expertise and ethical standards.

2. Experience: Choose someone with experience in your industry. They'll understand the specific financial challenges and opportunities your business faces.

Building a Collaborative Relationship

1. Communication: Maintain open and regular communication with your financial adviser or accountant. Share your business goals and any changes that might impact your financial strategy.

2. Trust: Trust is crucial. Ensure that you feel comfortable and confident in their advice and decisions.

Imagine navigating a complex maze. Without a map (financial adviser), you might hit dead ends and waste time. With the right guide, you move confidently, knowing you'll reach your destination with fewer headaches and more success.

"A good financial plan is a road map that shows us exactly how the choices we make today will affect our future."

– Alexa Von Tobel.

Investor Relations

Building Trust and Transparency: Investor relations are like a high-stakes dating game – you need to woo investors, build trust, and maintain a transparent relationship. Investors want to know their money is in safe, capable hands.

1. Clear Communication: Keep your investors informed about your business's performance, milestones, and challenges. Regular updates can be through newsletters, reports, or meetings.

2. Transparency: Be honest about your financial status and future prospects. Investors appreciate candor and are more likely to support you through ups and downs.

Effective Pitching

1. Know Your Audience: Tailor your pitch to your audience's interests and investment style. Some investors look for high-growth, while others seek stability.

2. Highlight Successes: Share your achievements and growth metrics. Showing a strong track record boosts investor confidence.

Engaging Investors

1. Personal Connections: Build personal relationships with your investors. Invite them to company events, share your vision, and listen to their feedback.

2. Thankfulness: Show appreciation for their support. A simple thank you can go a long way in maintaining goodwill.

Investor meetings can sometimes feel like trying to impress your in-laws. You put on your best suit, rehearse your lines, and hope they'll see the potential in your "baby" (business). And just like family gatherings, a little charm and honesty go a long way.

Exit Strategies

1. Planning for the Future: An exit strategy is like planning your retirement – you need a solid plan to ensure a smooth transition when it's time to step away from your business.

2. Types of Exit Strategies: Common exit strategies include selling your business, merging with another company, going public through an IPO, or passing the business to a family member.

3. Timing: The timing of your exit is crucial. You want to sell or exit when your business is at its peak value, not during a downturn.

Preparing for the Exit

1. Valuation: Get a professional valuation to understand your business's worth. This helps in negotiations and ensures you get a fair deal.

2. Documentation: Keep thorough records and documentation. Potential buyers will conduct due diligence, and well-organized records facilitate this process.

Ensuring a Smooth Transition

1. Succession Planning: If you plan to pass the business to a family member or employee, ensure they are well-prepared to take over.

2. Communication: Clearly communicate your plans to employees, customers, and stakeholders to maintain trust and continuity.

Planning an exit strategy is like preparing for a grand vacation. You've built your itinerary (plan), packed your bags (prepared your business), and now you just need to ensure everything goes smoothly so you can enjoy your "retirement" on a beach somewhere.

> *"In preparing for battle, I have always found that plans are useless, but planning is indispensable."*
>
> – Dwight D. Eisenhower.

Case Studies and Success Stories

Learning from Others: Case studies and success stories provide real-world examples of businesses that have navigated the start-up journey successfully. These stories offer valuable lessons and inspiration.

1. Highlighting Successes: Learn stories of businesses that started small and grew into industry leaders. Focus on key decisions, strategies, and turning points.

2. Learning from Failures: Read some case studies of businesses that faced challenges and overcame them. Failure is a part of the entrepreneurial journey, and these stories provide practical insights.

Case studies should sometimes read like a detective story. You follow the clues (decisions), uncover hidden motives (strategies), and celebrate when the mystery (success) is solved.

CHAPTER

V

BUILDING AND LEADING YOUR TEAM

The Importance of a Strong Team

Building Your Business Dream Team: Imagine you're assembling a superhero squad. Batman might be cool on his own, but without the Justice League, he's just a rich guy in a bat suit. Similarly, your business needs a strong team to soar to new heights. A cohesive team is the backbone of any successful start-up. They bring diverse skills, ideas, and perspectives that fuel innovation and drive growth.

1. Shared Vision and Goals: A strong team aligns with your company's vision and goals. They understand the mission and work toward it with enthusiasm.

2. Collaboration and Innovation: With the right mix of talent, your team can brainstorm innovative solutions and collaborate effectively to overcome challenges.

3. Resilience in Tough Times: A supportive team stands by each other during tough times, helping the company navigate through difficulties with strength and unity.

Building a start-up without a strong team is like trying to play a rock concert solo. Sure, you might be able to play a few instruments, but without the drummer, bassist, and lead guitarist, you're just a guy making noise in his garage. Remember, even The Beatles had Ringo!

> *"Great things in business are never done by one person;*
> *they're done by a team of people."*
>
> – Steve Jobs.

Identifying the Right Talent

The Talent Hunt: Finding the right talent is like dating – you swipe right on candidates who seem like a good fit, but it takes time to find the perfect match. The right team members are out there waiting to be discovered, and they're essential to transforming your vision into reality.

1. Skills and Experience: Look for candidates with the skills and experience relevant to your industry and business needs. But remember, skills can be taught; a great attitude and cultural fit are priceless.

2. Cultural Fit: Ensure candidates align with your company's values and culture. They should blend well with your existing team and add to the positive work environment.

3. Passion and Drive: Look for individuals who are passionate about their work and driven to succeed. They'll bring energy and motivation to the team.

Hiring the right talent can sometimes feel like a game of Where's Waldo. You sift through a sea of resumes, hoping to spot that one standout individual who perfectly fits your team. And just like Waldo, the right person might be hiding in plain sight!

"Hire character. Train skill."

– Peter Schutz, former CEO of Porsche

Crafting Job Descriptions

The Art of the Job Description: Writing job descriptions is like crafting a dating profile – you need to be clear, attractive, and honest to attract the right candidates. A well-crafted job description not only outlines the role but also sells your company to potential employees.

1. Clear and Concise Titles: Use straightforward job titles that accurately reflect the role. Avoid jargon or overly creative titles that might confuse candidates.

2. Detailed Responsibilities: Clearly outline the key responsibilities and expectations of the role. Be specific about the day-to-day tasks and long-term goals.

3. Required Skills and Qualifications: List the essential skills and qualifications needed for the role. Separate must-haves from nice-to-haves to avoid deterring potential candidates who may be a great fit.

4. Company Culture and Benefits: Highlight your company culture, values, and the benefits you offer. Give candidates a glimpse into what makes your company a great place to work.

Crafting a job description without scaring off potential candidates is a fine art. It's like advertising a haunted house: you want to thrill and excite, not send them running for the hills with tales of 'unlimited unpaid overtime.'

"Find a job you enjoy doing, and you will never have to work a day in your life."

– Mark Twain.

By emphasizing the importance of a strong team, guiding readers in identifying the right talent, and helping them craft compelling job descriptions, you'll keep your audience engaged while providing them with practical, actionable advice. Plus, a dash of humor and relatable scenarios will make the journey all the more enjoyable.

Effective Recruitment Strategies

The Quest for Talent: Recruiting the right talent can feel like searching for a needle in a haystack, but with effective strategies, you can turn that haystack into a goldmine. Finding the perfect candidates involves a mix of creativity, persistence, and a bit of luck.

1. Leverage Social Media and Professional Networks: Use platforms like LinkedIn, Twitter, and even Instagram to find and engage with potential candidates. Post about job openings and company culture to attract talent.

2. Employee Referrals: Your current employees can be your best recruiters. They know the company culture and can recommend people who would be a good fit. Plus, offering referral bonuses adds a fun twist!

3. Recruitment Agencies and Job Fairs: Partnering with recruitment agencies or attending job fairs can help you tap into a wider talent pool. It's like speed dating but for job seekers and employers.

4. Internship Programs: Establishing internship programs can help you identify and train future employees. It's a great way to test the waters before making long-term commitments.

Recruiting can sometimes be like fishing. You throw out a wide net (job postings) and hope to catch a big one (the perfect candidate). Just remember, if you catch a boot, it's time to change the fishing spot!

> *"Recruiting should be viewed as a business partner, someone who is critical to the success of the business."*
>
> – Mathew Caldwell.

Interview Techniques

The Art of the Interview: Conducting interviews is like being on a first date – you need to make a good impression, ask the right questions, and figure out if there's a future together. Effective interviewing helps you uncover the real potential of candidates.

1. Prepare Thoroughly: Review the candidate's resume and have a list of questions ready. Tailor your questions to the specific role and the candidate's background.

2. Behavioral Questions: Ask questions that reveal how candidates have handled situations in the past. For example, "Tell me about a time when you had to solve a difficult problem at work."

3. Assess Cultural Fit: Besides skills and experience, assess if the candidate aligns with your company culture. Questions about their values and work style can provide insights.

4. Two-Way Communication: Remember, interviews are a two-way street. Give candidates the opportunity to ask questions and discuss their expectations and aspirations.

Interviewing without preparation is like going on a blind date without knowing anything about the person – awkward silences and missed connections. But with a little homework, you can create a meaningful and productive conversation.

> *"The secret of my success is that we have gone to exceptional lengths to hire the best people in the world."*
>
> – Steve Jobs.

Onboarding New Employees

Welcome Aboard! - Onboarding new employees is like hosting a welcome party – you want to make them feel at home, introduce them to everyone, and ensure they have everything they need to start contributing. A smooth onboarding process sets the tone for their entire journey with your company.

1. Pre-Onboarding Preparation: Before the new hire's first day, ensure their workspace is ready and all necessary equipment is set up. Send them a welcome email with details about their first day.

2. First Day Essentials: Introduce the new hire to the team, provide a company tour, and explain the company's history, mission, and values. Make them feel part of the family.

3. Mentorship Programs: Pair new hires with a mentor or buddy who can guide them through the initial days. This helps them acclimate faster and provides a go-to person for questions.

4. Training and Development: Provide comprehensive training on their role and responsibilities. Outline clear goals and expectations and offer resources for ongoing learning and development.

Starting a new job without proper onboarding is like being dropped into a foreign country without a map. Sure, you might find your way eventually, but wouldn't it be nice to have a guide?

> *"Train people well enough so they can leave, treat them well enough so they don't want to."*
>
> – Richard Branson

Building a Positive Company Culture

The Heartbeat of Your Business: Creating a positive company culture is like hosting the ultimate party where everyone feels welcome, valued, and excited to be there. A vibrant culture not only attracts top talent but also keeps employees happy and productive.

1. Core Values: Define and communicate your company's core values. These should reflect what your business stands for and guide daily operations.

2. Inclusive Environment: Foster an environment where everyone feels included and respected. Diversity and inclusion lead to richer ideas and more innovative solutions.

3. Open Communication: Encourage open and transparent communication. Regular team meetings and feedback sessions help keep everyone on the same page.

4. Recognition and Rewards: Recognize and reward employees for their hard work and achievements. It doesn't always have to be monetary – even a simple shoutout can boost morale.

Creating a positive culture without understanding your employees is like trying to throw a surprise party for someone you barely know. Sure, everyone loves cake, but what if they're gluten-free?

"Culture eats strategy for breakfast."

– Peter Drucker.

Motivating Your Team

Lighting the Fire Within Motivating your team is like being a cheerleader and coach rolled into one. You need to inspire, support, and sometimes give a little pep talk to keep the momentum going.

1. Set Clear Goals: Establish clear, achievable goals. When employees know what they're working toward, they're more motivated to get there.

2. Empower Employees: Give your team the autonomy to make decisions and take ownership of their work. Empowered employees are more engaged and motivated.

3. Positive Reinforcement: Use positive reinforcement to encourage desired behaviors. A little praise can go a long way in boosting morale and motivation.

4. Professional Growth: Provide opportunities for professional development. When employees see a path for growth, they're more likely to stay motivated and loyal.

Motivating a team is like trying to get a cat to take a bath – sometimes, you need to be creative and patient. You can't just throw them in; you need to make them feel like it's their idea.

> *"People often say that motivation doesn't last.*
> *Well, neither does bathing – that's why we recommend it daily."*
>
> – Zig Ziglar.

PART - IX

Developing Leadership Skills

Becoming the Leader, Your Team Deserves: Developing leadership skills is like training for a marathon – it takes time, dedication, and a lot of practice. Great leaders aren't born; they're made through experience, learning, and growth.

1. Self-awareness: Understand your strengths and weaknesses. Self-aware leaders can leverage their strengths and work on improving their weaknesses.

2. Effective Communication: Develop strong communication skills. Good leaders listen as much as they speak and can convey their vision clearly.

3. Empathy and Emotional Intelligence: Show empathy and develop emotional intelligence. Understanding and connecting with your team on an emotional level builds trust and respect.

4. Decision-Making: Hone your decision-making skills. Being able to make informed and timely decisions is crucial for effective leadership.

5. Lead by Example: Set a positive example for your team. Your actions speak louder than words, and your team will follow your lead.

Developing leadership skills is like learning to juggle while riding a unicycle – it's challenging, but once you get the hang of it, you'll amaze everyone, including yourself.

> *"Before you are a leader, success is all about growing yourself.*
> *When you become a leader, success is all about growing others."*
>
> – Jack Welch.

Delegating Effectively

The Art of Letting Go: Delegating effectively is like being a chef in a busy kitchen – you can't cook every dish yourself, so you need to trust your sous chefs to handle the heat. Mastering the art of delegation is crucial for any leader.

1. Know Your Team's Strengths: Understand the strengths and weaknesses of your team members. Delegate tasks that align with their skills and expertise.

2. Set Clear Expectations: Clearly communicate what you expect from the task. Provide all necessary information and resources to ensure success.

3. Trust and Empower: Trust your team to get the job done. Micromanaging not only frustrates them but also defeats the purpose of delegation.

4. Provide Support: Be available for guidance and support without taking over. Encourage questions and provide constructive feedback.

5. Acknowledge Efforts: Recognize and appreciate the efforts of your team. A simple thank you can go a long way in motivating them.

Delegating without clear instructions is like asking your friend to pick up groceries without giving them a list. You might end up with ice cream and chips when you need eggs and milk – not the worst outcome, but not quite what you had in mind.

> *"Deciding what not to do is as important as deciding what to do."*
>
> – Jessica Jackley.

Team-Building Activities

Bonding Beyond the Desk: Team-building activities are like the glue that holds your team together. They foster camaraderie, enhance communication, and build trust among team members.

1. Icebreaker Games: Start with simple icebreakers like "Two Truths and a Lie" or "Human Knot" to get everyone relaxed and talking.

2. Outdoor Adventures: Plan outdoor activities like hiking, ropes courses, or scavenger hunts. These experiences challenge your team and promote teamwork.

3. Workshops and Seminars: Host workshops on skills development or fun topics like cooking or painting. Learning together can be a great bonding experience.

4. Volunteer Together: Organize community service projects. Working together for a good cause can strengthen team bonds and boost morale.

5. Office Fun: Create opportunities for fun in the office, like themed dress up days, trivia contests, or board game afternoons.

Team-building activities are like a high school group project, but fun – no one wants to do all the work, but when everyone pitches in, it's amazing how much you can achieve (and how much fun you can have).

"Coming together is a beginning. Keeping together is progress. Working together is a success."

– Henry Ford.

Managing Remote Teams

Leading from Afar: Managing remote teams is like being the captain of a ship in uncharted waters. You need clear communication, trust, and a strong sense of direction to keep everyone on course.

1. Set Clear Goals and Expectations: Define clear goals and expectations for your remote team. Use tools like project management software to keep track of progress.

2. Effective Communication: Utilize various communication tools like video calls, chat platforms, and emails to stay connected. Regular check-ins are essential.

3. Foster a Sense of Belonging: Create opportunities for remote team members to connect and bond. Virtual team-building activities and informal chats can help.

4. Provide the Right Tools: Ensure your team has access to the necessary tools and technology to perform their tasks efficiently.

5. Trust and Accountability: Trust your team to do their job and hold them accountable for their work. Focus on outcomes rather than micromanaging their every move.

Managing a remote team without clear communication is like trying to herd cats over a video call – chaotic, frustrating, and not very productive. But with the right approach, it can be as smooth as a cat nap.

> *"Remote work is not a privilege; it's a discipline.*
> *It's about creating a culture of trust, autonomy, and accountability."*
>
> – Wade Foster

Performance Management

Keeping the Engine Running Smoothly: Performance management is like tuning a high-performance car – regular maintenance and fine-tuning keep it running smoothly and efficiently. It's about setting clear expectations, providing feedback, and fostering growth.

1. Set Clear Objectives: Clearly define performance goals and expectations. Use SMART goals – Specific, Measurable, Achievable, Relevant, and Time-bound.

2. Regular Feedback: Provide regular, constructive feedback. Focus on both strengths and areas for improvement to help employees grow.

3. Performance Reviews: Conduct formal performance reviews periodically. These should be comprehensive and based on documented evidence.

4. Recognition and Rewards: Recognize and reward high performers. This can boost morale and motivate others to strive for excellence.

5. Professional Development: Offer opportunities for professional development. Encourage employees to enhance their skills and knowledge.

Managing performance without feedback is like trying to bake a cake without tasting the batter. You might end up with something that looks good but tastes terrible.

"The only way to do great work is to love what you do."

– Steve Jobs.

Conflict Resolution

Turning Heat into Light: Conflict resolution is like being a firefighter – you need to extinguish the flames before they spread and cause more damage. It's about addressing issues promptly and finding amicable solutions.

1. Address Issues Early: Don't let conflicts fester. Address issues as soon as they arise to prevent them from escalating.

2. Active Listening: Listen to all parties involved. Understanding different perspectives is crucial to finding a fair solution.

3. Remain Neutral: Stay neutral and avoid taking sides. Your role is to mediate and facilitate a resolution.

4. Find Common Ground: Identify common interests and goals. This helps in finding a solution that everyone can agree on.

5. Follow-Up: After resolving the conflict, follow-up with the involved parties. Ensure that the solution is working and that there are no residual issues.

Resolving conflicts without proper communication is like trying to solve a puzzle with missing pieces – frustrating and nearly impossible. But with a little patience and understanding, you can fit everything together nicely.

"Conflict is inevitable, but combat is optional."

– Max Lucado.

Encouraging Innovation and Creativity

Sparking the Genius Within: Encouraging innovation and creativity is like planting a garden – you provide the right conditions, and soon enough, you'll see a bloom of new ideas and solutions. It's about fostering an environment where creativity can thrive.

1. Create a Safe Space: Foster an environment where employees feel safe to share their ideas without fear of ridicule or rejection.

2. Encourage Experimentation: Allow your team to experiment and take calculated risks. Not all ideas will succeed, but failures can lead to valuable insights.

3. Diverse Teams: Build diverse teams with different backgrounds and perspectives. Diversity breeds creativity.

4. Provide Resources: Offer the necessary tools and resources for innovation. This includes time, technology, and training.

5. Celebrate Creativity: Recognize and reward creative efforts. Celebrating successes and learning from failures encourages a culture of innovation.

Encouraging creativity in a stifling environment is like asking a fish to climb a tree – it's just not going to happen. Give your team the right conditions, and they'll surprise you with their ingenuity.

"Innovation distinguishes between a leader and a follower."

– Steve Jobs.

Continuous Learning and Development

Embracing the Growth Mindset: Continuous learning and development are like upgrading your software – it keeps your skills sharp and your mind agile. In the fast-paced world of entrepreneurship, staying ahead means never stopping learning.

1. Embrace Lifelong Learning: Encourage your team (and yourself!) to continuously seek new knowledge and skills, whether it's through courses, workshops, or reading; every bit of learning counts.

2. Learning from Mistakes: Embrace failures as learning opportunities. As they say, the master has failed more times than the beginner has even tried.

3. Promoting a Learning Culture: Foster an environment where curiosity is encouraged, and mistakes are seen as stepping stones to success. It's not about being perfect; it's about progressing.

Continuous learning is like trying to keep up with the latest smartphone updates – just when you think you've mastered it, there's a new version with even more features you didn't know you needed.

"Education is the kindling of a flame, not the filling of a vessel."

– Socrates.

Succession Planning

Passing the Torch: Succession planning is like grooming the next quarterback – you're preparing someone to lead the team when you're no longer in the game. It ensures continuity and prepares your business for the future.

1. Identifying Future Leaders: Identify potential successors early on and invest in their development. It's like planting seeds for a fruitful harvest.

2. Knowledge Transfer: Document critical knowledge and skills. Make sure that important information doesn't walk out the door when someone leaves.

3. Building Leadership Bench Strength: Develop a pipeline of talent. Succession planning isn't just about replacing a leader; it's about nurturing a pool of capable leaders.

Succession planning without preparation is like trying to change a tire without a spare – you might get stuck on the side of the road. Plan ahead, and you'll always have a smooth ride.

> *"Succession planning is not just a strategy.*
> *It's an insurance policy for the long-term survival of your business."*

Handling Team Expansion

Growing Pains: Handling team expansion is like planting a garden – you need the right conditions for growth, or your plants (and team members) won't thrive. It's about scaling your team while maintaining cohesion and efficiency.

1. Strategic Hiring: Hire for fit as well as skill. You're not just adding bodies; you're adding to your team culture.

2. Onboarding and Integration: Smooth onboarding is key. Think of it like welcoming a new family member – you want them to feel at home from day one.

3. Communication and Alignment: As your team grows, communication becomes even more critical. Keep everyone aligned with your vision and goals.

Handling team expansion is like playing Tetris – you're constantly rearranging and adjusting to fit everything together perfectly. Sometimes, you need to rotate a few pieces to make it work.

"Alone we can do so little; together we can do so much."

– Helen Keller.

Balancing Work-Life Integration

Finding Harmony: Balancing work-life integration is like juggling – you have multiple balls in the air, and dropping one can throw everything off. It's about finding harmony between your professional and personal life.

1. Setting Boundaries: Define clear boundaries between work and personal time. It's okay to unplug and recharge.

2. Flexibility and Adaptability: Embrace flexibility in how, when, and where work gets done. It's about focusing on results rather than hours clocked.

3. Self-Care: Prioritize self-care and well-being. A burned-out entrepreneur isn't effective. Take breaks, exercise, and do things that recharge you.

Balancing work and life is like spinning plates – sometimes one wobbles, but with a little finesse, you can keep them all in the air (most of the time).

"Work to live, don't live to work."

CHAPTER
VI
MARKETING AND SALES STRATEGIES

The Foundations of Effective Marketing

Building the Bedrock of Your Business: Imagine marketing as the foundation of a house. Without a solid base, your beautifully designed rooms (products) won't stand a chance. Effective marketing is the cornerstone that supports and promotes your business.

1. Understanding Marketing Fundamentals: At its core, marketing is about communication. It's how you tell the world who you are, what you offer, and why you're the best choice.

2. The 4 Ps of Marketing: Product, Price, Place, and Promotion. These are your guiding stars, helping you navigate the marketing landscape. Ignore them at your peril!

3. Consistency is Key: Your messaging needs to be consistent across all channels. Think of it like a catchy jingle – if it's stuck in people's heads, you're doing it right.

"Marketing without data is like driving with your eyes closed." - Dan Zarrella. Imagine driving a car with a blindfold – thrilling for a movie, disastrous for your business.

> *"Doing business without advertising is like winking at a girl in the dark.*
> *You know what you are doing, but nobody else does."*
>
> – Stuart H. Britt.

Understanding Your Target Market

Getting to Know Your Audience: Understanding your target market is like dating. You wouldn't propose on the first date (unless you're starring in a rom-com). You need to understand what makes your audience tick.

1. Market Research: Dive deep into demographics, psychographics, and behaviors. Know their likes, dislikes, habits, and fears. Stalk them – but in a legal, data-driven way.

2. Creating Buyer Personas: Develop detailed profiles of your ideal customers. Give them names, backstories, and personalities. Meet Sally, the eco-conscious millennial who loves yoga and hates plastic.

3. Customer Segmentation: Break your market into segments. It's like sorting M&Ms by color – it helps you understand and cater to each group's unique tastes.

Understanding your target market is like understanding your spouse. Ignore their needs and interests, and you'll be in the doghouse. Listen and cater to them, and you're a hero.

> *"Your customer doesn't care how much you know until*
> *they know how much you care."*

> – Damon Richards.

Crafting a Compelling Value Proposition

Why Should They Choose You? - Your value proposition is your elevator pitch – if you had only 30 seconds to tell someone why they should pick you, what would you say? Make it count!

1. Identify Your Unique Selling Points (USPs): What makes you different? Why should they care? It's like being the only ice cream truck in a desert – make it obvious why they need you.

2. Communicate Benefits, Not Features: Focus on how your product improves their life. Instead of saying, "Our vacuum has 1200 watts of power," say, "Our vacuum leaves your home spotless in minutes."

3. Keep It Simple and Clear: Your value proposition should be easily understood. If you need a thesaurus to decipher it, you've gone too far.

Crafting a value proposition is like trying to impress a date in 30 seconds. You want to highlight your best qualities without sounding like you're bragging.

> *"People don't buy what you do; they buy why you do it."*
>
> – Simon Sinek.

Building Your Brand Identity

Who Are You, Really? - Building your brand identity is like picking out your outfit for the biggest party of the year. It's how you present yourself to the world and make a lasting impression.

Defining Your Brand's Personality: Is your brand fun and quirky or serious and professional? Imagine your brand as a person. How would they talk, dress, and interact with others?

Creating a Visual Identity: Your logo, colors, and design elements should reflect your brand's personality. Think of it as your brand's wardrobe – it should be stylish, cohesive, and recognizable.

Crafting Your Brand Voice: This is how your brand speaks to its audience. Is it formal or casual? Witty or straightforward? Consistency is key – you don't want to sound like Shakespeare one day and a stand-up comedian the next.

Building your brand identity is like trying to choose a profile picture for a dating app. You want to look good, stand out, and reflect your true self – without the filters.

"Your brand is what other people say about you when you're not in the room."

– Jeff Bezos.

Creating a Marketing Plan

Your Roadmap to Success - Creating a marketing plan is like planning a road trip. You need a map, a destination, and plenty of snacks – I mean, strategies.

1. Setting Clear Objectives: What do you want to achieve? More sales? Greater brand awareness? Set SMART goals (Specific, Measurable, Achievable, Relevant, Time-bound).

2. Defining Your Strategies and Tactics: How will you reach your goals? Break it down into actionable steps. Think of it as your itinerary – where are you going, and how will you get there?

3. Allocating Your Budget: Determine how much you're willing to spend and allocate it wisely. Remember, you don't want to blow your budget on the first leg of the trip and be stuck hitchhiking the rest of the way.

Creating a marketing plan is like preparing for a zombie apocalypse. You need a plan, the right tools, and a backup strategy because things rarely go as expected.

"By failing to prepare, you are preparing to fail."

– Benjamin Franklin.

Digital Marketing Essentials

Navigating the Online World: Digital marketing is like navigating a bustling city. There are countless paths to take, but only some will lead you to your destination.

1. Website Optimization: Your website is your digital storefront. Make sure it's inviting, easy to navigate, and optimized for search engines. No one wants to shop in a messy store or one that's hard to find.

2. Content Marketing: Create valuable, engaging content that resonates with your audience. Think of it as giving free samples – if they like what they taste, they'll come back for more.

3. Social Media Strategies: Use social media to connect with your audience, share your story, and build your brand. Remember, it's called social media for a reason – be social!

4. Email Marketing: Stay in touch with your customers through regular, personalized emails. It's like sending a friendly postcard – just make sure it's not spammy!

5. SEO and SEM: Help people find you online through search engine optimization and marketing. It's like putting up a giant neon sign that says, "We're here! Come check us out!"

Digital marketing is like trying to get your cat's attention. You need to be engaging, consistent, and sometimes a little sneaky to get them to notice you.

"Content is fire; social media is gasoline."

– Jay Baer.

Leveraging Influencers and Ambassadors

The Power of Word-of-Mouth on Steroids: Leveraging influencers and ambassadors is like having a popular friend who always talks you up at parties. They boost your credibility and widen your reach.

1. Identifying the Right Influencers: Not all influencers are created equal. Look for those who align with your brand values and have an engaged audience. Think quality over quantity – it's better to have a few true fans than a million passive followers.

2. Building Relationships: Treat influencers as partners, not just marketing tools. Engage with them authentically, and they'll be more likely to promote your brand genuinely. It's like making a friend – showing interest and appreciation.

3. Creating Engaging Campaigns: Work with influencers to develop creative, engaging campaigns that resonate with their audience. Remember, if it's fun for them, it's likely to be fun for their followers too.

Leveraging influencers is like having your cool older cousin take you to the school dance. Suddenly, everyone wants to know you and be your friend.

> *"Influence is not about convincing people to like you.*
> *It's about making people feel they are missing out if they don't."*

Paid Advertising Strategies

Investing in Visibility: Paid advertising is like buying a megaphone to shout your message in a crowded marketplace. Done right, it amplifies your voice above the noise.

1. Choosing the Right Platforms: Determine where your audience spends their time. Whether it's Google Ads, Facebook, or LinkedIn, ensure your message is where it will be seen.

2. Crafting Compelling Ads: Your ads should grab attention and drive action. Use strong visuals, clear messages, and irresistible calls-to-action. Think of it like a flashy billboard – eye-catching and to the point.

3. Measuring and Optimizing: Track your ad performance and tweak as needed. It's like seasoning a dish – keep tasting and adjusting until it's just right.

Paid advertising is like fishing with a net instead of a hook. You cast a wide reach, but you still need the right bait to catch the right fish.

"Stopping advertising to save money is like stopping your watch to save time."

– Henry Ford.

Public Relations: Building Credibility

Getting the Right Kind of Attention: Public relations (PR) is about building and maintaining a positive image. It's like being the charming guest at a dinner party – everyone remembers you for the right reasons.

1. Crafting Your Story: Develop a compelling narrative about your brand. What's your origin story? What are your values? Share your journey and connect emotionally with your audience.

2. Media Relations: Build relationships with journalists and media outlets. Provide them with interesting stories and newsworthy updates. It's like befriending the gossip columnist – get them on your side, and they'll spread the word.

3. Handling Crises: Be prepared for the inevitable hiccup. Respond quickly, transparently, and positively. It's like spilling wine on the host's carpet – handle it gracefully, and people will remember your recovery, not the spill.

PR is like hosting a dinner party. You want everyone to have a great time and leave talking about how fabulous the evening was – even if you burned the main course.

"PR is performance recognition. You don't buy it; you earn it."

– Douglas Smith.

PART - X

Networking and Relationship Building

The Art of Making Connections: Networking and relationship building is like planting seeds in a garden. With time and care, they grow into fruitful relationships that benefit both parties.

1. The Importance of Networking: Building a strong network can open doors to opportunities and collaborations. It's not about the number of contacts you have but the quality of those relationships.

2. Effective Networking Strategies: Attend industry events, join professional groups, and leverage social media to connect with like-minded individuals. Think of it as attending a party where you genuinely want to get to know people, not just collect business cards.

3. Maintaining Relationships: Follow-up and stay in touch. Send a quick message, share useful information, or arrange a coffee meeting. It's like nurturing a plant – consistent care yields the best results.

Networking is like speed dating – you have a short time to make a memorable impression, so bring your best self and a dash of charm.

"Your network is your net worth."

– Porter Gale.

Sales Funnels and Lead Generation

Guiding Prospects to Become Customers: Creating effective sales funnels and generating leads is like setting up a series of dominos. Each step should naturally lead to the next, culminating in a successful sale.

1. Understanding the Sales Funnel: From awareness to interest, decision, and action, map out the journey your customers take. It's like planning a road trip – you need a clear route to your destination.

2. Lead Generation Techniques: Use content marketing, social media, email campaigns, and SEO to attract potential customers. Think of it as casting a wide net to catch the most promising leads.

3. Nurturing Leads: Engage with your leads through personalized communication and valuable content. It's like dating – keep them interested and invested in the relationship until they're ready to commit.

Generating leads is like fishing. You need the right bait, a good spot, and a lot of patience. Just don't fall asleep with the rod in your hand!

> *"A sales funnel is like a first date. If you only talk about yourself,*
> *there won't be a second one."*

– Steli Efti.

Closing the Sale: Techniques that Work

Sealing the Deal: Closing a sale is the final, crucial step in the sales process. It's like crossing the finish line in a race – exhilarating and rewarding.

1. Understanding Customer Needs: Listen to your customers and address their concerns. It's like being a detective – the more you know, the better you can solve their problem.

2. Building Trust: Establish credibility and demonstrate the value of your product or service. Trust is the currency of sales – without it, the deal falls apart.

3. Effective Closing Techniques: Use strategies like the assumptive close, the urgency close, or the value summary close. It's like picking the right tool for the job – each situation may require a different approach.

Closing a sale is like proposing marriage. You've put in the time and built the relationship, and now it's time to pop the question – just don't be surprised if you hear a "let me think about it."

"You don't close a sale; you open a relationship if you want to build a long-term, successful enterprise."

– Patricia Fripp.

Customer Relationship Management (CRM)

Cultivating Lasting Connections: Customer Relationship Management (CRM) is like maintaining a great friendship. You keep track of important details, celebrate milestones, and always show that you care.

1. Understanding CRM: CRM involves managing your company's interactions with current and potential customers. It's the secret sauce that keeps customers happy and coming back.

2. Choosing the Right CRM System: There are many CRM tools available, from simple spreadsheets to sophisticated software. Choose one that fits your business needs. Think of it like picking the right shoes – they need to fit well and be comfortable for the long haul.

3. Maximizing CRM Benefits: Use CRM to track customer interactions, sales, and service requests. It's like having a photographic memory – you'll never forget a customer's preferences or purchase history.

CRM is like your mom reminding you about your cousin's birthday. It helps you stay on top of things and make people feel special.

"Customer service shouldn't just be a department;
it should be the entire company."

– Tony Hsieh.

Data-Driven Marketing Decisions

Making Informed Choices: Data-driven marketing is like having a GPS for your business. It shows you the best route to take, avoiding traffic jams and detours.

1. The Importance of Data: Data helps you understand customer behavior, market trends, and campaign effectiveness. It's like having a crystal ball – you can predict the future and adjust your strategy accordingly.

2. Collecting and Analyzing Data: Use tools like Google Analytics, social media insights, and CRM reports. It's like being a detective – gather clues, analyze patterns, and solve the mystery of what your customers want.

3. Applying Insights: Make informed decisions based on data to optimize your marketing efforts. It's like cooking – follow the recipe (data), and you're more likely to end up with a delicious result.

Using data in marketing is like trying to bake a cake without a recipe. Sure, you might get something edible, but it probably won't taste very good.

"In God we trust, all others bring data."

– W. Edwards Deming.

Analyzing Marketing Metrics

Measuring What Matters: Analyzing marketing metrics is like checking your fitness tracker. You need to know how well you're doing and where you can improve.

1. Key Metrics to Track: Monitor metrics like conversion rates, customer acquisition costs, and return on investment. These are your vital signs – keep an eye on them to ensure your business is healthy.

2. Using Tools and Dashboards: Tools like Google Analytics, HubSpot, and Tableau can help visualize your data. It's like having a dashboard in your car – you can see all the important information at a glance.

3. Making Data-Driven Adjustments: Use your metrics to tweak campaigns and strategies. It's like tuning a musical instrument – small adjustments can lead to a perfect performance.

Analyzing metrics without acting on them is like going to the gym and just watching other people exercise. You need to do something with that information!

"If you can't measure it, you can't improve it."

– Peter Drucker.

Adapting to Market Changes

Staying Nimble in a Dynamic World: Adapting to market changes is like surfing – you have to be ready to ride the waves and change direction as needed.

1. Embracing Change: Markets evolve, and businesses must stay flexible. Adaptability is key to survival and success. Think of it as being a chameleon – blend in with your surroundings to stay relevant.

2. Monitoring Market Trends: Keep an eye on industry news, competitor movements, and customer feedback. It's like being a weather forecaster – you need to predict storms and sunny days to plan accordingly.

3. Implementing Changes: When market conditions shift, adjust your strategies, products, and services. It's like upgrading your wardrobe – you need to dress appropriately for the season.

Adapting to market changes is like trying to follow the latest dance craze. Just when you've mastered the Macarena, everyone's doing the Floss.

> *"It is not the strongest of the species that survive, nor the most intelligent, but the one most responsive to change."*
>
> – Charles Darwin.

Building a Community Around Your Brand

Creating Loyal Followers: Building a community around your brand is like hosting a great party – everyone feels welcome, engaged, and eager to come back.

1.   Engaging with Your Audience: Use social media, forums, and events to interact with your customers. It's like being the life of the party – get everyone talking and having a good time.

2.   Creating Valuable Content: Share stories, tips, and behind-the-scenes looks to build a sense of belonging. It's like telling campfire stories – make them memorable and engaging.

3.   Encouraging User-Generated Content: Let your community contribute reviews, photos, and testimonials. It's like hosting a potluck dinner – everyone brings something to the table, making it a richer experience for all.

Building a community is like throwing a party. You can't just invite people and hope they'll have fun. You need good music, great snacks, and a host who knows how to keep the conversation flowing.

> *"People don't buy what you do; they buy why you do it.*
> *And what you do simply proves what you believe."*

> – Simon Sinek

Harnessing the Power of Testimonials and Reviews

Turning Customer Praise into Gold: Testimonials and reviews are like the applause at the end of a performance – they show that your audience appreciates what you do.

1. Collecting Testimonials: Ask satisfied customers for feedback and permission to share their experiences. It's like getting letters of recommendation – they add credibility to your claims.

2. Showcasing Reviews: Highlight positive reviews on your website, social media, and marketing materials. It's like framing and hanging up your diploma – it shows you've earned your place.

3. Responding to Feedback: Engage with both positive and negative reviews. Thank your supporters and address concerns promptly. It's like hosting a Q&A session after a show – it shows you care about your audience's experience.

Harnessing testimonials is like having your mom brag about you to her friends. It's more believable coming from someone else, even if you're pretty great!

"Your brand is what other people say about you when you're not in the room."

– Jeff Bezos

Event Marketing and Webinars

Connecting with Your Audience: Event marketing and webinars are like throwing a grand celebration – you bring people together, share valuable experiences, and leave a lasting impression.

1. The Power of Live Events: Hosting live events allows you to interact with your audience in real-time, creating a deeper connection. Think of it as a rock concert – the energy and excitement are palpable.

2. Planning and Promoting Events: From securing a venue to spreading the word, effective event planning is crucial. It's like organizing a wedding – every detail matters to ensure a memorable experience.

3. Engaging Webinars: Webinars provide a platform to educate and interact with a global audience. It's like hosting a virtual dinner party – keep it lively, informative, and interactive.

Hosting a webinar is like trying to keep a classroom full of kindergartners engaged over Zoom. You need tricks up your sleeve to keep everyone's attention!

"Marketing is no longer about the stuff that you make,
but about the stories you tell."

– Seth Godin.

Collaborations and Partnerships

Strength in Numbers: Collaborations and partnerships are like forming a superhero team – you combine strengths to tackle challenges and achieve greater success.

1. Identifying Potential Partners: Look for businesses or individuals who complement your strengths and share your values. It's like finding the perfect dance partner – you need someone who moves in sync with you.

2. Creating Win-Win Partnerships: Ensure that both parties benefit from the collaboration. It's like a good marriage – both sides need to give and take to make it work.

3. Maintaining Strong Relationships: Keep communication open and regularly assess the partnership's effectiveness. It's like tending a garden – regular care and attention keep it flourishing.

Collaborations are like group projects in school. You hope everyone will pull their weight, but you always end up doing the lion's share of the work. Choose your partners wisely!

"Alone we can do so little; together we can do so much."

– Helen Keller.

Understanding Buyer Psychology

The Mind Behind the Purchase: Understanding buyer psychology is like playing a game of chess – anticipate the next move and plan your strategy accordingly.

1. The Decision-Making Process: Buyers go through stages before making a purchase: awareness, consideration, and decision. It's like planning a vacation – you research destinations, compare options and finally book the trip.

2. Emotional Triggers: Emotions play a significant role in purchasing decisions. Tap into feelings of happiness, security, and excitement. It's like a good rom-com – make them laugh, cry, and ultimately, fall in love.

3. The Power of Social Proof: People tend to follow the crowd. Highlight testimonials, reviews, and endorsements. It's like seeing a long line outside a restaurant – if everyone's going there, it must be good!

Understanding buyer psychology is like trying to figure out why your cat does what it does. It's often a mystery, but once you crack the code, you can predict their next move (and avoid getting scratched).

"People don't always buy what they need; they buy what they want."

– Zig Ziglar.

Sales Pitch Mastery

Nailing the Art of Persuasion: Mastering the sales pitch is like delivering a compelling monologue – you need to captivate your audience, keep them engaged, and leave them wanting more.

1. Knowing Your Audience: Tailor your pitch to the specific needs and interests of your audience. It's like preparing a custom-tailored suit – one size does not fit all.

2. Crafting a Clear and Concise Message: Get to the point quickly and clearly. Remember, attention spans are short – like trying to keep a toddler focused at story time.

3. Practicing Delivery: Rehearse your pitch until it flows naturally. Think of it as being an actor in a play – the more you practice, the more confident and convincing you become.

Giving a sales pitch is like trying to convince your friend to binge-watch your favorite TV series. You have to highlight the best parts, leave out the spoilers, and ensure that it's worth every minute.

"The best salespeople know that their expertise can become their enemy in selling. At the moment, they are tempted to tell the buyer what 'he needs to do,' but instead offer a story about a peer of the buyer."

– Mike Bosworth.

Developing a Unique Selling Proposition (USP)

Standing Out from the Crowd: Creating a USP is like designing your signature dish – it should be distinctive, memorable, and leave a lasting impression.

1. Identifying Your Unique Value: Determine what sets your product or service apart from the competition. It's like finding your secret sauce – what makes you irresistibly unique?

2. Communicating Benefits Clearly: Make sure your USP is simple and easy to understand. Think of it as writing a catchy slogan – it should stick in people's minds like a great jingle.

3. Aligning with Customer Needs: Ensure your USP addresses the specific desires and pain points of your target market. It's like matching a puzzle piece – it should fit perfectly into what your customers are looking for.

Developing a USP is like trying to stand out in a crowded room. You don't need to be the loudest person, just the most interesting one. Maybe you're the only one who brought cupcakes – everyone loves cupcakes.

"You have to be unique and different, and shine in your own way."

– Lady Gaga.

Storytelling for Sales Success

Weaving a Narrative that Sells: Storytelling in sales is like spinning a captivating yarn – it draws people in, engages their emotions, and makes your message unforgettable.

1. Crafting a Compelling Narrative: Use stories to illustrate the value and impact of your product. It's like writing a good novel – having a clear beginning, middle, and end that keeps readers hooked.

2. Using Real-Life Examples: Share testimonials and case studies to make your story relatable. It's like sharing a friend's experience – people trust and remember personal anecdotes.

3. Eliciting Emotions: Tap into the emotional side of your audience. Make them feel the problem and the relief your solution provides. It's like telling a fairy tale – make them feel the struggle and celebrate the victory.

Using storytelling in sales is like trying to get your kids to eat vegetables. You tell them about Popeye and how spinach made him strong – suddenly, those greens look a lot more appealing.

"Marketing is no longer about the stuff that you make,
but about the stories you tell."

– Seth Godin.

Building and Training a Sales Team

Crafting Your Sales Dream Team: Building a sales team is like assembling a superhero squad – each member should have unique strengths that contribute to the overall mission.

1. Recruiting the Right Talent: Look for individuals with diverse skills and a passion for sales. Think of it as casting for a blockbuster movie – you need both the charming lead and the strategic mastermind.

2. Comprehensive Training Programs: Provide thorough training to ensure everyone is on the same page. It's like training a sports team – practice makes perfect, and everyone needs to know the plays.

3. Fostering a Positive Team Culture: Create an environment where team members support each other. It's like hosting a dinner party – everyone should feel welcome and valued.

Building a sales team is like putting together a band. You need a charismatic lead singer, a steady drummer, and don't forget the bass player – the unsung hero who holds it all together.

> *"Great things in business are never done by one person;*
> *they're done by a team of people."*
>
> – Steve Jobs.

Creating Irresistible Offers

Crafting Deals That Can't Be Refused: Creating offers that your customers can't resist is like baking a cake – you need the right ingredients, timing, and presentation.

1. Understanding Customer Needs: Know what your customers truly want and tailor your offers accordingly. It's like knowing your audience's favorite dessert – you wouldn't serve a pie to a cake lover.

2. Adding Value: Include extras that enhance the perceived value of your offer. Think of it as adding sprinkles to your ice cream – a little something extra makes it even more appealing.

3. Time-Sensitive Promotions: Create a sense of urgency to encourage quick decisions. It's like announcing a limited-time sale – who can resist a ticking clock?

Creating irresistible offers is like trying to get your dog to take a bath. Sometimes, you have to hide the medicine in a treat – they'll never see it coming.

> *"Offer them what they secretly want, and they, of course,*
> *immediately become panic-stricken."*
>
> – Jack Kerouac.

Overcoming Sales Objections

Turning 'No' into 'Yes': Handling sales objections is like playing chess – you need to anticipate moves and plan your strategy carefully.

1. Listening Actively: Understand the root of the objection by listening carefully. It's like being a detective – the clues are in what they're not saying as much as what they are.

2. Empathizing with Concerns: Show empathy and address their worries sincerely. It's like comforting a friend – sometimes, they just need to know you understand.

3. Providing Solutions: Offer clear, convincing solutions to overcome their objections. It's like fixing a flat tire – once the problem is solved, the journey continues smoothly.

Handling sales objections is like negotiating with a toddler at bedtime. You need patience, creativity, and, sometimes, a willingness to concede that one extra story.

"You don't close a sale; you open a relationship
if you want to build a long-term, successful enterprise."

– Patricia Fripp.

The Art of Negotiation

Mastering the Dance of Deals: Negotiation is like a dance – it requires rhythm, finesse, and the occasional twirl to reach a harmonious agreement.

1. Preparing for Negotiations: Research your counterpart and understand their needs and priorities. It's like studying your dance partner's moves before hitting the floor.

2. Setting Clear Objectives: Know your limits and what you aim to achieve. It's like deciding your dance routine – know your steps, but be ready to improvise.

3. Maintaining Composure: Stay calm and composed during negotiations, even if things get tricky. It's like dancing through a surprise thunderstorm – keep your cool, and you'll still shine.

Negotiating is like trying to decide toppings on a pizza with friends – everyone has their preferences, and you hope no one orders pineapple.

"The most difficult thing in any negotiation, almost, is making sure that you strip it of the emotion and deal with the facts."

– Howard Baker.

Utilizing Marketing Automation Tools

Efficiency in Every Click: Marketing automation is like having a personal assistant who never sleeps – it handles repetitive tasks so you can focus on the big picture.

1. Automating Routine Tasks: Schedule emails, social media posts, and follow-ups automatically. It's like having a robot that knows your schedule better than you do.

2. Segmenting Your Audience: Target specific groups with personalized messages. It's like inviting friends to different parties – each group gets the right invitation.

3. Analyzing Campaign Performance: Use data to refine your strategies and improve results. It's like checking the scoreboard during a game – you adjust your plays based on what's working.

Using marketing automation is like having a magic wand – it turns mundane tasks into effortless spells that attract customers.

> *"Automation and technology don't solve problems;*
> *they amplify existing approaches."*

– Sam Woods.

Building an Online Presence

Claiming Your Digital Territory: Building an online presence is like constructing a skyscraper – it requires a solid foundation, careful planning, and constant maintenance.

1. Creating a Professional Website: Your website is your virtual storefront. It's like dressing up for a first date – make a good impression, and they'll want to come back.

2. Engaging on Social Media: Interact with your audience and share valuable content regularly. It's like hosting a party – keep the conversation flowing and make everyone feel welcome.

3. Optimizing for Search Engines: Use SEO strategies to increase visibility online. It's like being on a treasure hunt – you want to be the hidden gem that everyone discovers.

Building an online presence is like trying to find your way in a new city using GPS – you might take a wrong turn or 2, but eventually, you find your place.

"Social media is not just an activity; it is an investment of valuable time and resources. Surround yourself with people who not just support you and stay with you, but inform your thinking about ways to WOW your online presence."

– Sean Gardner

Customer Acquisition vs. Retention Strategies

Finding and Keeping Your Tribe: Customer acquisition and retention is like juggling – you need the right balance to keep your business thriving.

1. Customer Acquisition Strategies: Think of it as fishing – you cast your net wide to attract new customers. Use targeted advertising, promotions, and compelling offers to reel them in.

2. Retention Tactics: Once you catch them, think of retention as nurturing a garden – you cultivate loyalty through exceptional service, personalized experiences, and loyalty programs.

3. Balancing Act: It's like dating – you want to attract new suitors while making your current partner feel special. Keep the romance alive with surprises and genuine connections.

Customer acquisition is like speed dating – you have a short time to impress and convince them you're the best choice.

> *"Acquiring a new customer is much more expensive than retaining an existing one."*

> – Amy Gallo.

Handling Customer Complaints and Feedback

Turning Lemons into Lemonade: Handling customer complaints is like defusing a bomb – approach it calmly, deftly, and with a strategy to defuse the situation.

1. Listening with Empathy: Hear them out, understand their frustration, and acknowledge their feelings. It's like being a therapist – sometimes, they just need to vent.

2. Taking Swift Action: Resolve issues promptly and effectively. It's like putting out a fire – the quicker you act, the less damage it causes.

3. Learning and Improving: Use feedback to improve your products or services. It's like getting free advice – valuable insights that can lead to better business decisions.

Handling customer complaints is like being a referee in a game – you aim to make fair calls and ensure everyone leaves satisfied, even if they didn't win.

"Your most unhappy customers are your greatest source of learning."

– Bill Gates.

Leveraging Analytics for Better Insights

Data-Driven Decision-Making: Leveraging analytics is like having a crystal ball – it helps you predict trends, understand customer behavior, and make informed decisions.

1. Collecting the Right Data: It's like being a detective – gather clues (data) that lead to solving the case (understanding customer needs).

2. Analyzing Trends: Look for patterns and insights that can guide your strategies. It's like reading tea leaves – find the patterns that predict future outcomes.

3. Driving Action: Use data to optimize campaigns, personalize experiences, and maximize ROI. It's like having a map – it shows you the best route to reach your destination.

Leveraging analytics is like navigating a maze – with the right data, you find the shortest path to success without hitting dead ends.

"Data beats emotions."

– Sean Rad.

Trends and Innovations in Marketing and Sales

Riding the Wave of Change: Staying ahead in marketing and sales is like surfing – you need to catch the right wave (trends) and balance to stay on top of the competition.

1. Embracing Digital Transformation: It's like upgrading from a flip phone to a smartphone – adapt to new technologies like AI, AR, and VR for more engaging customer experiences.

2. Personalization Revolution: Think of it as being a tailor-made message and offers that fit each customer perfectly, like a bespoke suit.

3. Content is King (and Queen): Creating valuable content is like hosting a dinner party – serve up something delightful that keeps guests (your audience) coming back for more.

Following trends in marketing is like keeping up with fashion – sometimes, last season's trend is this season's faux pas.

"The best marketing doesn't feel like marketing."

– Tom Fishburne.

Case Studies of Successful Marketing Campaigns

Learning from the Masters: Studying successful marketing campaigns is like dissecting magic tricks – you want to uncover the secrets behind the awe-inspiring results.

1. Nike's 'Just Do It' Campaign: It's like a motivational coach – inspiring millions to push their limits with a simple slogan.

2. Coca-Cola's Share a Coke Campaign: Think of it as a friend offering a drink – personalizing products to connect emotionally with consumers.

3. Apple's 'Get a Mac' Ads: Like a comedy duo – using humor to highlight product superiority and win hearts.

Studying successful marketing campaigns is like binge-watching a TV series – you can't stop until you know how it ends (and what made it so successful).

"Good marketing makes the company look smart.
Great marketing makes the customer feel smart."

– Joe Chernov.

Future-Proofing Your Marketing Strategy

Preparing for Tomorrow's Challenges: Future-proofing your marketing strategy is like building a spaceship – anticipate future landscapes and equip yourself with the right tools and strategies.

1. AI and Machine Learning: It's like having a marketing assistant who never sleeps – analyze data, predict trends, and personalize experiences.

2. Voice Search Optimization: Think of it as learning a new language – optimize for conversational queries to stay relevant in the age of voice assistants.

3. Sustainability and Ethics: Like planting a tree – consumers are increasingly eco-conscious, so align your brand with sustainable practices that resonate.

Future-proofing your marketing strategy is like playing chess against a supercomputer – think several moves ahead and be ready to adapt to unexpected moves.

"Marketing is no longer about the stuff that you make, but about the stories you tell."

– Seth Godin.

CHAPTER

VII

PRODUCT DEVELOPMENT AND LAUNCH

Idea Generation and Validation

Spark Your Inner Innovator: Generating ideas is like fishing – you cast your net wide to catch the big one that's both innovative and market-worthy.

1. Brainstorming Sessions: It's like a comedy improv – no bad ideas, just stepping stones to the great ones.

2. Market Research: Think of it as detective work – uncovering clues (customer needs and preferences) to crack the case (perfect product idea).

3. Validation Process: Like a reality check – ensuring your idea isn't just a wild dream but something customers will eagerly embrace.

Idea generation is like planting seeds in a garden – nurture them well, and they'll grow into something amazing; neglect them, and they might turn into weeds.

"Innovation distinguishes between a leader and a follower."

– Steve Jobs.

Prototyping and Iterative Design

Building Castles in the Air: Prototyping and iterative design are like sculpting – shaping raw materials into a masterpiece through continuous refinement.

1. Creating the Blueprint: It's like drafting architectural plans – mapping out each detail before construction begins.

2. Prototype Development: Think of it as crafting a rough draft – testing ideas and making adjustments until you find the perfect fit.

3. Iterative Refinement: Like polishing a gem – each iteration brings you closer to a product that shines.

Prototyping is like baking a cake – the first attempt might be a disaster, but with each adjustment, it gets closer to perfection.

"Prototyping is the conversation you have with your ideas."

– Tom Wujec.

User-Centered Design

Designing for Delight: User-centered design is like throwing a surprise party – it's all about making your customers feel special and understood.

1. Empathy Mapping: It's like stepping into someone else's shoes – understanding their needs, desires, and pain points.

2. Feedback Loops: Think of it as a dialogue – listening attentively to customer input and incorporating it into your design.

3. Usability Testing: Like hosting a focus group – observing how users interact with your product to refine its usability.

User-centered design is like cooking for friends – you want them to enjoy every bite and come back for seconds.

"Design is not just what it looks like and feels like. Design is how it works."

– Steve Jobs.

Minimum Viable Product (MVP)

Dipping Your Toes In Launching a Minimum Viable Product (MVP) is like testing a new recipe – start with the basics, adjust flavors based on feedback, and avoid serving a half-baked dish.

1. Core Features Only: Think of it as a starter pack – enough to showcase your idea without overwhelming your customers.

2. Speed to Market: Like preparing a quick meal – get your product out there fast to gauge interest and iterate swiftly.

3. Iterative Improvement: It's like adding seasoning – each iteration makes your product tastier (or, in this case, more appealing to users).

Launching an MVP is like test-driving a car with 3 wheels – it gets you where you need to go, but you're eager to add that fourth wheel for a smoother ride.

"The best way to predict the future is to create it."

– Peter Drucker

Beta Testing and Feedback Loops

Let the Feedback Flood In Beta testing and feedback loops are like hosting a focus group – listen attentively to what your early users have to say and use their insights to refine your product.

1. Engaging Early Adopters: Think of it as inviting friends to a potluck – their feedback helps you fine-tune the recipe (your product) before the big dinner (official launch).

2. Bug Squashing: Like exterminating pests – address issues swiftly to ensure a smooth user experience.

3. Feature Prioritization: It's like choosing toppings for a pizza – focus on what your users crave the most to deliver maximum satisfaction.

Beta testing is like planting seeds – nurture your testers well, and they'll help your product grow; neglect them, and they might not sprout enthusiasm.

"Your most unhappy customers are your greatest source of learning."

– Bill Gates.

Scalability Planning

Growing Pains: Planning for scalability is like building a skyscraper – lay a strong foundation, but also design for future floors without causing structural collapse.

1. Infrastructure Readiness: Think of it as upgrading from a garden hose to a fire hydrant – prepare your systems to handle increased demand.

2. Team Expansion: Like hiring new chefs for a bustling restaurant – scale your team to match growing production needs.

3. Maintaining Quality: It's like baking cookies – ensure each batch tastes as good as the first, even as you bake more.

Scaling a business is like inflating a balloon – do it too fast, and you might pop too slow, and you risk falling behind competitors.

"Growth is never by mere chance; it is the result of forces working together."

– James Cash Penney.

Cross-Functional Collaboration

Teamwork Makes the Dream Work: Cross-functional collaboration is like a relay race – each team member passes the baton smoothly to achieve a common goal without dropping it.

1. Breaking Silos: It's like knocking down walls between departments – fostering communication and synergy.

2. Ideation Sessions: Think of it as a brainstorming potluck – everyone brings their best dish (ideas) to create a feast of innovation.

3. Project Management: Like conducting an orchestra – ensuring every instrument (team) plays in harmony to produce a masterpiece (product).

Cross-functional collaboration is like organizing a surprise party – each team member has a role to play, and if one person spills the beans (fails to communicate), the surprise is ruined.

"Alone we can do so little; together we can do so much."

– Helen Keller.

Brand Alignment and Product Identity

Staying True to Your Colors: Brand alignment and product identity is like maintaining a signature style – whether you're dressing up for a gala or designing a product, consistency is key to leaving a lasting impression.

1. Brand Guidelines: Think of it as a fashion designer's sketchbook – outlining colors, fonts, and messaging to maintain brand integrity.

2. Visual Storytelling: Like painting a masterpiece – every brushstroke (design element) contributes to the overall narrative (brand story).

3. Customer Perception: It's like curating an art exhibit – ensure every piece (product) reflects the brand's values and resonates with your audience.

Brand alignment is like singing karaoke – you want to hit the right notes (brand message) and keep the audience (customers) singing along.

"Your brand is what other people say about you when you're not in the room."

– Jeff Bezos

Market Readiness

Seize the Moment: Market readiness is like surfing – catching the right wave (launch timing) can propel you forward, while missing it could leave you paddling back to shore.

1. Competitive Analysis: Think of it as sizing up your opponents – understanding market trends and timing your move strategically.

2. Customer Demand: Like reading tea leaves – interpret signals (customer feedback and behavior) to predict the best time to launch.

3. Marketing Campaign Timing: It's like launching fireworks – timing the ignition to dazzle your audience and maximize impact.

Launching a product is like making pancakes – the first one might be a bit lopsided, but with practice (timing adjustments), you'll flip them perfectly every time.

"The future depends on what you do today."

– Mahatma Gandhi.

Launch Strategies and Tactics

Setting the Stage for Success: Launching a product is like planning a blockbuster movie release – it requires careful strategy, anticipation, and a touch of showmanship.

1. Preparation Phase: It's like assembling a puzzle – laying out all the pieces (marketing, logistics, team readiness) to create a clear picture of success.

2. Target Audience Engagement: Think of it as inviting guests to a party – create buzz, intrigue, and excitement to ensure a full house on launch day.

3. Campaign Execution: Like conducting a symphony – every instrument (marketing channel) plays its part to harmonize and captivate your audience.

Launching a product is like trying to fold a fitted sheet – it seems daunting at first, but with practice (strategy and planning), you can master it.

"Plans are nothing; planning is everything."

– Dwight D. Eisenhower.

Post-Launch Evaluation and Adaptation

The Aftermath: Learning from Launch: Post-launch evaluation is like analyzing a football game – reviewing plays (metrics and feedback) to see what worked, what didn't, and how to improve for the next match.

1. Analyzing Metrics: Think of it as decoding a secret message – uncover insights (sales data, customer feedback) to refine your strategy.

2. Customer Feedback: Like reading reviews – listen attentively to what your audience is saying to adjust your product and messaging accordingly.

3. Iterative Improvement: It's like fine-tuning a recipe – make adjustments to ensure your product evolves with market demands and customer preferences.

Post-launch evaluation is like cooking a meal – taste-testing to see if you need more spice (engagement) or less salt (refinements) for the perfect dish (product).

"Every day is a new day. It is better to be lucky. But I would rather be exact. Then when luck comes, you are ready."

– Ernest Hemingway.

Handling Unexpected Challenges

Expecting the Unexpected: Handling unexpected challenges is like navigating a maze – twists, turns, and surprises require agility, creativity, and sometimes a bit of luck.

1. Problem-Solving Mindset: Think of it as playing chess – strategize your moves (solutions) carefully to overcome obstacles.

2. Team Collaboration: Like a relay race – pass the baton (issues) between team members, each contributing their expertise to reach the finish line (solution).

3. Adaptability: It's like being a chameleon – adjust your approach swiftly in response to changing circumstances to maintain momentum.

Handling unexpected challenges is like juggling flaming torches – keep your cool, stay focused, and try not to set anything (or anyone) on fire.

"In the middle of difficulty lies opportunity."

– Albert Einstein

Case Studies of Successful Product Launches

Learning from the Pros: Studying successful product launches is like dissecting a magic trick – understanding the mechanics behind the illusion (strategy, timing, execution) reveals the secrets to captivating an audience.

1. Apple's iPhone Launch: Imagine unveiling a new gadget – the suspense, the hype, and the seamless integration of technology that leaves everyone buzzing for more.

2. Tesla's Model S: It's like driving into the future – sleek design, innovative features, and a sustainable edge that redefines the automotive industry.

3. Coca-Cola's New Coke Fiasco: Sometimes even giants stumble – exploring how a misstep (launching New Coke) turned into a lesson in listening to customer feedback and swift recovery.

Studying successful product launches is like binge-watching a TV series – each episode (launch) leaves you on the edge of your seat, eager to see what happens next.

"Success leaves clues."

– Tony Robbins.

The Role of Storytelling in Product Launches

Painting a Picture with Words: Storytelling in product launches is like crafting a captivating novel – weaving together characters (brand, product), plot (benefits, features), and setting (market context) to engage readers (customers) from beginning to end.

1. Creating Emotional Connections: It's like composing a symphony of emotions – using narratives to resonate with your audience and inspire action.

2. Building Anticipation: Imagine setting the stage – each chapter (teaser, sneak peek) builds suspense, leading to an unforgettable climax (launch day).

3. Brand Identity Reinforcement: It's like writing your brand's autobiography – every story (campaign, messaging) reinforces who you are and why you matter.

Storytelling in product launches is like telling a ghost story – it's not just about scaring your audience but also leaving them with a lingering sense of wonder and excitement.

"Stories create community, enable us to see through the eyes of other people, and open us to the claims of others."

– Peter Forbes.

Ethical Considerations in Product Development

Doing Well by Doing Good: Ethical considerations in product development are like navigating a moral compass – ensuring decisions (from sourcing to marketing) align with values that benefit both customers and society.

1. Sustainable Practices: It's like planting seeds – cultivating products and practices that nurture the planet and future generations.

2. Consumer Trust: Imagine building a house of cards – each ethical decision (transparency, fairness) strengthens the foundation of trust with your audience.

3. Social Responsibility: It's like being a good neighbor – contributing positively to communities and supporting causes that matter beyond profit margins.

Ethical considerations in product development are like choosing toppings for a pizza – it's not just about what tastes good, but also what's good for you and everyone at the table.

"Ethics is knowing the difference between what you have a right to do and what is right to do."

– Potter Stewart.

VIII

OPERATIONS AND SCALING

Streamlining Processes for Efficiency

Mastering the Art of Smooth Sailing: Streamlining processes for efficiency is like conducting an orchestra – every instrument (task) plays its part in harmony to create a symphony of productivity.

1. Identifying Bottlenecks: It's like playing detective – uncovering where time (and sanity) disappear faster than socks in a dryer.

2. Implementing Lean Principles: Think of it as Marie Kondo-ing your workflow – keeping only what sparks joy (efficiency) and discarding the rest.

3. Continuous Improvement: It's like upgrading your phone – regular updates (process tweaks) ensure you're always running at optimal speed.

Streamlining processes is like assembling IKEA furniture – confusing at first, but once you get the hang of it (efficiency hacks), it all comes together beautifully.

"Efficiency is doing things right; effectiveness is doing the right things."

– Peter Drucker.

Automation: The Future of Operations

Embracing the Rise of Machines: Automation in operations is like having a robot assistant – handling repetitive tasks so you can focus on the creative (and fun) aspects of your job.

1. From R2-D2 to Jarvis: Imagine having a helpful sidekick – automating tasks like data entry and scheduling to free up your time for strategic planning.

2. AI and Machine Learning: It's like having a crystal ball – predicting trends (customer behavior, market shifts) to stay one step ahead of the competition.

3. Integration Across Departments: Think of it as a dance party – each department (marketing, sales, operations) syncing their moves (data sharing) for a seamless experience.

Automation is like teaching a dog to fetch – with the right training (software setup), it becomes your loyal assistant, always ready to fetch (data and insights).

"Automation applied to an inefficient operation will magnify the inefficiency."

– Bill Gates.

Scaling without Compromise

Growing Pains, Managed: Scaling without compromise is like riding a bike uphill – challenging, but with the right gears (strategies), you can conquer any slope (growth phase) without losing balance.

1. Maintaining Quality: It's like baking a cake – ensuring each layer (product, service) meets the same delicious standard, no matter how big the cake gets.

2. Customer-Centric Scaling: Think of it as expanding a family business – keeping the warmth and personalized touch (customer service) even as you grow.

3. Scaling Culture: It's like planting a garden – nurturing values (team spirit, innovation) that bloom even as your company branches out.

Scaling without compromise is like teaching a whale to tap dance – it's about finding the right rhythm (balance between growth and quality) without making waves.

"Scaling a business is not just about growing bigger; it's about growing better. True success lies in maintaining the integrity of your mission and the quality of your offerings, even as you expand."

– Adapted from McKinsey.

Logistics and Supply Chain Management

Navigating the Highway of Delivery: Logistics and supply chain management are like orchestrating a ballet of packages – ensuring each pirouette (delivery) is flawless and on time, without any unexpected twirls.

1. Efficient Routing: It's like playing Tetris with trucks – finding the perfect fit (route) to maximize efficiency and minimize delays.

2. Inventory Control: Think of it as playing Jenga – balancing stock levels to keep the tower (supply chain) stable without collapsing.

3. Last-Mile Delivery: It's like delivering pizza – ensuring the final stretch (from warehouse to doorstep) is as speedy and satisfying as possible.

Logistics and supply chain management are like planning a road trip with friends – you want everything to go smoothly, but there's always that one unexpected detour (supply chain hiccup).

"The supply chain is like nature; it is all around us."

– Tim Cook.

Lean Principles for Start-Ups

Trimming the Fat for Agility: Applying lean principles in start-ups is like Marie Kondo-ing your workspace – keeping only what sparks joy (value) and discarding the rest to create a clutter-free (efficient) environment.

1. Eliminating Waste: It's like cleaning out your closet – removing unnecessary steps (processes) to streamline operations and maximize productivity.

2. Kaizen (Continuous Improvement): Think of it as leveling up in a video game – small, incremental improvements (tweaks in processes) that lead to significant gains over time.

3. Flexible Manufacturing: It's like a LEGO set – assembling your production process in modular pieces so you can adapt quickly to changing demands.

Applying lean principles in start-ups is like going on a diet – you shed the excess (inefficiencies) to become lean and mean (competitive) without sacrificing your favorite snacks (core strengths).

"Perfection is achieved not when there is nothing more to add, but when there is nothing left to take away."

– Antoine de Saint-Exupery.

Customer-Centric Operations

Putting Customers in the Spotlight: Customer-centric operations are like hosting a dinner party – anticipating needs, providing exceptional service, and ensuring everyone leaves with a smile (positive experience).

1. Personalized Service: It's like having a personal concierge – tailoring interactions (support, recommendations) to each customer's preferences.

2. Feedback Loop: Think of it as a two-way street – listening attentively (surveys, reviews) and responding promptly to enhance satisfaction and loyalty.

3. Building Relationships: It's like nurturing a friendship – cultivating trust and loyalty through meaningful interactions (communication, support).

Customer-centric operations are like remembering everyone's favorite dessert at a potluck – it's not just about meeting expectations but exceeding them in delightful ways.

"Your most unhappy customers are your greatest source of learning."

– Bill Gates.

Scaling Customer Support

Growing Pains, Happy Customers: Scaling customer support is like adding extra seats to a magic show – ensuring every guest (customer) feels like they have front-row access to your stellar service.

Investing in Technology: It's like upgrading from a bicycle to a spaceship – using AI and chatbots to handle routine inquiries while your human support team focuses on more complex magic tricks (issues).

Training and Empowerment: Think of it as coaching a sports team – equipping your support champions (team members) with the skills and confidence to handle any curveball (customer query).

Maintaining Personal Touch: It's like hosting a family reunion – ensuring even as you grow, each customer feels valued and part of your close-knit (customer service) family.

Scaling customer support is like a circus performance – you want to juggle multiple tasks (queries) with finesse without dropping any balls (customer satisfaction).

"Customer service shouldn't just be a department,
it should be the entire company."

– Tony Hsieh.

Risk Management in Operations

Navigating Stormy Seas: Risk management in operations is like sailing a ship – predicting storms (challenges) and navigating safely to your destination (success) with a sturdy vessel (strategic planning).

1. Identifying Risks: It's like playing detective – uncovering potential hazards (market shifts, supply chain disruptions) before they rock your boat (business).

2. Mitigation Strategies: Think of it as building a fortress – implementing safeguards (protocols, redundancies) to protect your treasure (business assets) from pirates (risks).

3. Adaptability and Flexibility: It's like being a superhero – ready to pivot (adjust strategies) at a moment's notice to overcome unexpected villains (crises).

Risk management is like preparing for a surprise party – you want to have contingencies in place (backup plans) in case the unexpected guest (challenge) shows up early.

> *"In preparing for battle, I have always found that plans are useless,*
> *but planning is indispensable."*

> – Dwight D. Eisenhower.

Crisis Management and Business Continuity Planning

When the Going Gets Tough: Crisis management and business continuity planning are like being the conductor of an orchestra during a surprise blackout – keeping the music (operations) going smoothly despite the chaos.

1. Response Protocols: It's like rehearsing for a play – ensuring every team member knows their role (responsibilities) when the curtain unexpectedly falls.

2. Communication Strategies: Think of it as playing telephone – ensuring clear and timely updates (internal and external) to maintain trust and confidence.

3. Learning from Crises: It's like a superhero origin story – every crisis (challenge) is an opportunity to emerge stronger and more resilient.

Crisis management is like surviving a zombie apocalypse – you need a solid plan (strategy), quick reflexes (decisiveness), and a sense of humor to stay sane amidst the chaos.

"In the middle of every difficulty lies opportunity."

– Albert Einstein

Monitoring and Metrics

Numbers Tell a Story: Monitoring and metrics are like having a crystal ball – using data to uncover hidden insights and guide your business decisions with Jedi-like precision.

1. Key Performance Indicators (KPIs): It's like tracking your fitness progress – focusing on metrics (customer satisfaction, sales growth) that matter most to your business health.

2. Real-Time Analytics: Think of it as playing chess – making strategic moves (adjustments in marketing, operations) based on real-time data to stay ahead of your competition.

3. Continuous Improvement: It's like leveling up in a video game – using insights (metrics) to tweak your strategies and unlock new achievements (business milestones).

Monitoring and metrics are like reading tea leaves – interpreting trends (data) to predict the future (business outcomes) with a mix of science and intuition.

"Without data, you're just another person with an opinion."

– W. Edwards Deming.

CHAPTER

IX

RESILIENCE AND CONTINUOUS IMPROVEMENT

The Power of Resilience

Bouncing Back Stronger: Resilience in entrepreneurship is like being a rubber band – the ability to stretch without breaking and snap back into shape after facing challenges that would make a lesser band give up and fly across the room.

1. Embracing Setbacks: It's like hitting every red light on your way to an important meeting – frustrating at the moment, but a chance to practice patience and find alternative routes.

2. Turning Adversity into Advantage: Think of it as making lemonade out of the lemons life gives you – using setbacks as fuel to propel you forward rather than letting them sour your spirits.

3. Perseverance Pays Off: Resilience is like running a marathon – it's not just about starting strong, but about enduring through the tough stretches and crossing the finish line with pride.

Resilience is like trying to fold a fitted sheet – it seems impossible at first, but with patience and a few deep breaths, you manage to tame the chaos and end up with a neatly folded sheet (and a sense of accomplishment).

> *"The greatest glory in living lies not in never falling,*
> *but in rising every time we fall."*

– Nelson Mandela.

Learning from Failure

Failing Forward: Failure in entrepreneurship is like a crash landing – it's not the end of the journey, but a chance to inspect the damage, learn from the experience, and take off again with a stronger plan.

1. Embracing the Lessons: It's like trying a new recipe and burning the dish – you learn what not to do next time and maybe discover a unique smoky flavor no one expected.

2. Resilience in Rejection: Think of it as auditioning for a play and not getting the lead role – it stings, but it's an opportunity to refine your performance and try out for the next production.

3. Failure as Fuel for Success: Learning from failure is like refining gold – it's a process of heating, hammering, and polishing until you uncover the valuable lessons hidden within.

Failure is like tripping on a banana peel – embarrassing at the moment, but if you can laugh it off and learn to watch your step, you'll avoid slipping up next time.

"Success is not final, failure is not fatal: It is the courage to continue that count."

– Winston Churchill.

Adaptability in a Changing Landscape

Rolling with the Punches: Adaptability in entrepreneurship is like dancing in a flash mob – staying in sync with the ever-changing rhythm of market trends and customer demands while keeping your unique groove.

1. Spotting Trends Early: It's like being a detective – noticing subtle clues (market shifts, technological advancements) that hint at where the dance floor (market) is headed next.

2. Flexibility in Strategy: Think of it as improvising a jazz solo – you have a framework (business plan), but you riff off it to create something fresh and exciting that resonates with your audience.

3. Embracing Innovation: Adaptability is like upgrading your smartphone – staying current with the latest features (innovations) while maintaining the core functionality (customer satisfaction).

Adaptability is like trying to fold a map – it's a bit outdated these days, but if you can navigate the twists and turns with a GPS (innovation), you'll reach your destination (success) faster.

> *"It is not the strongest of the species that survive,*
> *nor the most intelligent, but the one most responsive to change."*

– Charles Darwin.

Continuous Improvement as a Habit

Turning Good into Great: Continuous improvement in entrepreneurship is like upgrading your favorite app – always adding new features, fixing bugs, and making it smoother to use, ensuring it stays ahead of the competition.

1. The Kaizen Philosophy: It's like brushing your teeth – small, consistent efforts every day lead to healthier teeth (business) and a brighter smile (customer satisfaction).

2. Innovation as a Lifestyle: Think of it as renovating your home – you start with one room (product/service), but as you see what works and what doesn't, you refine and expand until your entire house shines.

3. Embracing Feedback: Continuous improvement is like tuning a guitar – you adjust the strings (business strategies) based on feedback until the melody (customer experience) resonates perfectly.

Continuous improvement is like learning to juggle – you drop the ball (make mistakes), but with practice and determination, you learn new tricks (improvements) that impress your audience.

"Strive for continuous improvement, instead of perfection."

– Kim Collins.

Feedback Loops and Iterative Development

Listen, Learn, Adapt: Feedback loops in entrepreneurship are like having a GPS in a maze – they guide you through twists and turns (customer insights), helping you navigate to the treasure (business success) faster and more efficiently.

1. Capturing Customer Insights: It's like fishing – casting your line (listening to feedback) and reeling invaluable insights (customer preferences) that help you catch the big fish (loyal customers).

2. Iterative Development: Think of it as sculpting – starting with a rough shape (initial product/service), but with each chisel (iteration based on feedback), refining until you create a masterpiece (market-leading solution).

3. Real-Time Adjustments: Feedback loops are like driving a car – you adjust your steering (business strategies) based on road conditions (market feedback) to ensure a smooth and safe journey (customer satisfaction).

Feedback loops are like trying on new clothes – you might need a few alterations (changes based on feedback) before the outfit (product/service) fits perfectly and makes you feel confident.

Your most unhappy customers are your greatest source of learning."

– Bill Gates.

Building Personal Resilience

Strength in Every Struggle: Building personal resilience in entrepreneurship is like training for a marathon – enduring the miles (challenges), strengthening your endurance (perseverance), and crossing the finish line (success) with grit and determination.

1. Managing Stress: It's like juggling – balancing multiple tasks (business demands) without dropping the ball (personal well-being) and learning to laugh when you inevitably fumble.

2. Embracing Setbacks: Building resilience is like climbing a mountain – the view (success) is breathtaking, but it's the climb (overcoming obstacles) that makes it truly rewarding.

3. Self-Care Strategies: Think of it as nurturing a garden – you need to water (self-care), prune (manage stress), and protect (embrace setbacks) your plants (personal resilience) to help them thrive.

Building resilience is like cooking a gourmet meal – you might burn a few dishes (make mistakes), but with practice and a dash of humor, you become a master chef (resilient entrepreneur).

"Life doesn't get easier or more forgiving, we get stronger and more resilient."

– Steve Maraboli.

Strategies for Overcoming Adversity

Navigating Stormy Seas: Overcoming adversity in entrepreneurship is like sailing through rough waters – adjusting your sails (strategies) to weather the storms (challenges) and steering toward calmer shores (success).

1.   Embracing Flexibility: It's like dancing in the rain – you might get wet (face challenges), but embracing the rhythm (flexibility) allows you to enjoy the dance (journey to success).

2.   Turning Setbacks into Comebacks: Overcoming adversity is like playing chess – you strategize (plan) your moves, anticipate setbacks (opponent's moves), and adapt your strategy (pivot) to stay ahead.

3.   Resilience as a Superpower: Think of it as building a skyscraper – each setback (challenge) is a brick (experience) that strengthens your foundation (resilience) and elevates you closer to the sky (success).

Overcoming adversity is like driving through traffic – you might hit a few red lights (obstacles), but with patience and a good playlist (positive attitude), you eventually reach your destination (goals).

"Success is not final, failure is not fatal: It is the courage to continue that count."

– Winston Churchill.

The Role of Mentorship and Support Networks

Guidance on the Journey: Mentorship and support networks in entrepreneurship are like having a compass and a map – they guide you through uncharted territories (challenges), provide insights (advice), and connect you with fellow travelers (network).

1. Learning from Experience: It's like having a GPS – mentors (guides) share their routes (experiences), helping you navigate shortcuts (tips) and avoid detours (mistakes) on your entrepreneurial journey.

2. Building a Safety Net: Think of it as a safety rope – support networks (mentors and peers) catch you when you stumble (face challenges), offering encouragement (support) to climb higher (achieve goals).

3. Pay It Forward: Mentorship is like planting a tree – you nurture saplings (mentees) with knowledge and care, knowing they'll grow strong (successful) and provide shade (support) for others in the future.

Mentorship is like learning to ride a bike – you might wobble (make mistakes) at first, but with a guiding hand (mentor), you gain confidence and pedal toward success.

"A mentor is someone who allows you to see the hope inside yourself."

– Oprah Winfrey.

Innovative Problem-Solving

Thinking Outside the Box: Innovative problem-solving in entrepreneurship is like solving a puzzle – exploring different pieces (strategies), finding the right fit (solution), and creating a picture (success) that inspires awe.

1. Embracing Creativity: It's like painting a masterpiece – blending colors (ideas), experimenting with strokes (approaches), and creating a canvas (solution) that captivates hearts (customer needs).

2. Iterative Experimentation: Think of it as cooking a new dish – you mix ingredients (strategies), taste-test (evaluate), and adjust the recipe (pivot) until you create a dish (solution) that delights taste buds (solves problems).

3. Turning Challenges into Opportunities: Innovative problem-solving is like a sculptor – you carve away obstacles (challenges), revealing a statue (opportunity) that stands tall (success) in the marketplace.

Innovative problem-solving is like playing charades – you act out different solutions (ideas), and when someone guesses right (finds the best solution), everyone cheers (celebrates success).

> *"Every problem is an opportunity in disguise."*
>
> – John Adams.

Measuring Resilience and Improvement

Quantifying the Journey: Measuring resilience and improvement in entrepreneurship is like tracking your fitness journey – recording milestones (achievements), analyzing progress (growth), and setting new goals (targets) to reach peak performance.

1. Defining Success Metrics: It's like playing a game – you set the rules (metrics), track points (progress), and strategize (improve) your gameplay (business) to win (succeed) in the long run.

2. Learning from Setbacks: Think of it as a science experiment – you hypothesize (strategies), experiment (implement), and analyze results (measure) to refine your approach and achieve breakthroughs (success).

3. Celebrating Small Wins: Measuring resilience and improvement is like climbing a mountain – you celebrate each step (progress), knowing that reaching the summit (ultimate goal) is a journey worth savoring.

Measuring resilience and improvement is like gardening – you plant seeds (goals), nurture growth (progress), and enjoy the harvest (success) with a sense of accomplishment.

> *"Measure what is measurable, and make measurable what is not so."*
>
> – Galileo Galilei.

X

FUTURE-PROOFING YOUR BUSINESS

Anticipating Market Trends and Disruptions

Anticipating market trends isn't just about predicting the future; it's about positioning yourself to capitalize on change before your competitors do. Whether it's the next big thing in technology or a shift in consumer behavior, staying ahead requires a keen eye and a willingness to adapt.

Imagine being able to predict the next viral TikTok trend or the emergence of a new technology that changes everything from how we shop to how we work. Anticipating market trends is like having a crystal ball, except instead of seeing mystical visions, you're analyzing data and reading the signs of the times.

"Predicting the future is easy.
It's trying to figure out what's going on now that's hard."

– Fritz Weaver.

There's excitement in being ahead of the curve but also a bit of nervousness. What if you miss the mark? What if your predictions fall flat? It's a rollercoaster of anticipation and anxiety, but that's what makes business thrilling.

"Change before you have to."

– Jack Welch

Innovation as a Core Strategy

Innovation isn't just about coming up with new ideas; it's about transforming those ideas into something that adds value to your customers and disrupts the status quo. It's the lifeblood of any successful business, fueling growth and staying power in a competitive landscape.

Think about the last time you encountered a product or service that made you say, "Wow, why didn't I think of that?" Innovation is about solving problems in ways that surprise and delight, leaving your competitors scrambling to catch up.

"Innovation is seeing what everybody has seen
and thinking what nobody has thought."

– Dr. Albert Szent-Györgyi.

There's a thrill in innovation, from the excitement of discovery to the satisfaction of seeing your ideas come to life. But there are also moments of doubt and frustration when things don't go as planned. It's a journey of highs and lows that tests your resilience and creativity.

"Innovation distinguishes between a leader and a follower."

– Steve Jobs.

Investing in Technology and Automation

Technology isn't just a tool; it's a game-changer that can revolutionize how you do business. From automating repetitive tasks to leveraging big data for insights, investing in technology isn't just about keeping up—it's about setting the pace.

Imagine a world where robots handle customer service; AI predicts market trends with eerie accuracy, and data analytics guides every decision. Investing in technology isn't just about staying relevant; it's about future-proofing your business and unlocking new possibilities.

"Before you become too entranced with gorgeous gadgets and mesmerizing video displays, let me remind you that information is not knowledge, knowledge is not wisdom, and wisdom is not foresight." - Arthur C. Clarke.

There's a sense of wonder in technology but also a fear of the unknown. Will AI take over our jobs? Can robots really replace human intuition? It's a balancing act between embracing progress and preserving what makes us uniquely human.

"The future belongs to those who prepare for it today."

– Malcolm X.

Adapting to Regulatory and Legal Changes

Navigating the labyrinth of regulatory and legal changes can feel like trying to solve a Rubik's cube blindfolded. From new data privacy laws to industry-specific regulations, staying compliant isn't just a necessity—it's a strategic advantage.

Imagine running a marathon where the finish line keeps moving. That's what it's like for businesses trying to keep up with regulatory changes. But instead of a medal, you get peace of mind knowing you're on the right side of the law.

"Lawyers are like beavers: They get in the mainstream and dam it up." - John Naisbitt.

There's frustration in deciphering legal jargon and fear of hefty fines for non-compliance. But there's also relief in knowing that staying ahead of regulations protects your business and builds trust with customers.

"Compliance is not just about playing defense. It's about playing offense, too."

– Julie Brill.

Diversifying Revenue Streams

Relying on a single revenue stream is like balancing on a tightrope without a safety net. Diversifying your revenue streams not only strengthens your financial stability but also opens doors to new opportunities and markets.

Imagine your business as a garden. Diversifying revenue streams is like planting different crops—some for immediate harvest, others for long-term growth. It's about hedging your bets and ensuring a bumper crop year after year.

*"Always look for new ways to increase your income because
you never know when the old ways might dry up."*

– H. Jackson Brown, Jr.

There's excitement in exploring new ventures and fear of stretching resources too thin. But there's also pride in building a resilient business model that can weather economic storms and seize opportunities.

"Never depend on a single income. Make investment to create a second source."

– Warren Buffett.

Building Resilience in Supply Chains

A supply chain is only as strong as its weakest link. Building resilience means fortifying your supply chain against disruptions, whether it's a global pandemic or a sudden spike in demand.

Imagine your supply chain as a game of Jenga. Each block represents a supplier or distributor. Building resilience means carefully balancing each block to withstand the unexpected tremors of the market.

> *"Supply chain disruptions are like unexpected guests—they can arrive at any time and wreak havoc."*

> – Anonymous.

There's anxiety in managing logistics and satisfaction in optimizing efficiency. But there's also camaraderie in collaborating with suppliers and relief in knowing your supply chain can adapt to unforeseen challenges.

> *"Resilience is all about being able to overcome the unexpected. Sustainability is about survival. The goal of resilience is to thrive."*

> – Jamais Cascio.

Sustainability and Corporate Responsibility

Sustainability isn't just a buzzword; it's a compass guiding businesses toward a future where profit meets planet and people. Embracing corporate responsibility isn't just about checking boxes; it's about making meaningful impacts that resonate with customers and communities.

Imagine your business as a steward of the planet, balancing profit with environmental stewardship. It's not just about reducing carbon footprints; it's about leaving a legacy of sustainability for generations to come.

"Going green is not just about recycling. It's about using the least amount of resources in the first place. So, next time, just take one napkin, not a whole stack!"

There's pride in adopting eco-friendly practices and anxiety about the daunting task of change. But there's also fulfillment in knowing your business is contributing positively to the world.

"The environment is where we all meet; where we all have a
mutual interest; it is the one thing all of us share."

– Lady Bird Johnson.

Strategic Partnerships and Alliances

In business, partnerships are like dance partners—they can make your moves more graceful or trip you up. Strategic partnerships and alliances are about finding the right rhythm and harmonizing strengths to achieve mutual success.

Imagine your business as a jazz band, where each instrument plays a unique role but together creates harmonious melodies. Strategic partnerships are like finding the perfect ensemble to make your business's song resonate louder and farther.

"Finding a good business partner is like finding a spouse:
you have to learn how to work together and love each other even
when you want to wring each other's necks."

– Lori Greiner.

There's excitement in exploring new collaborations and apprehension about sharing control. But there's also trust in knowing that strategic partnerships can open doors to new markets and innovations.

"Alone we can do so little; together we can do so much."

– Helen Keller.

PART - IX

Preparing for Economic Uncertainty

Economic uncertainty is like a roller coaster ride—thrilling at times but stomach-churning at others. Preparing for economic uncertainty isn't just about weathering storms; it's about building a resilient business model that can navigate choppy waters and emerge stronger.

Imagine your business as a sailor navigating unpredictable seas. Preparing for economic uncertainty is like stocking your ship with sturdy sails, provisions, and a skilled crew—ready to adjust course at a moment's notice.

> *"Economic forecasts may tell you a great deal about the forecaster;*
> *they tell you nothing about the future."*

– Warren Buffett.

There's fear in facing economic downturns and optimism in finding silver linings. But there's also wisdom in preparing for the unexpected and agility in seizing opportunities amid uncertainty.

> *"In times of economic uncertainty, the greatest danger is not turbulence;*
> *it's to act with yesterday's logic."*

– Peter Drucker.

Embracing Remote Work and Hybrid Models

Remote work isn't just a trend; it's a seismic shift in how businesses operate. Embracing remote work and hybrid models isn't just about adapting to circumstances; it's about embracing flexibility and empowering employees to thrive.

Imagine your business as a pioneer in the digital frontier, where physical boundaries dissolve and productivity soars. Embracing remote work and hybrid models is like unlocking a treasure trove of talent and innovation from anywhere on the map.

"Remote work: because pajamas are the new power suits."

There's liberation in escaping the daily commute and isolation in missing office camaraderie. But there's also inclusivity in accommodating diverse work styles and resilience in adapting to new norms.

"Remote work is the future of work."

– Alexis Ohanian.

End Note

There you have it—your journey from a flicker of an idea to a roaring success! Congratulations on reaching this milestone in your entrepreneurial adventure. As you reflect on the hurdles overcome and the triumphs celebrated, remember to savor the moments that define your path. Whether it was navigating the treacherous waters of market competition or mastering the art of the perfect elevator pitch, each experience has shaped you into the resilient entrepreneur you are today.

Throughout this book, we've shared laughs over the quirks of start-up life—like the mythical quest for the perfect office coffee machine or the strategic placement of post-it notes as reminders in a chaotic world. Humor has been our companion, reminding us to find joy in the journey, even when the spreadsheets threaten to take over.

But it hasn't all been smooth sailing. We've insight into the emotional rollercoaster of entrepreneurship—the exhilaration of landing that first big client, the nerve-racking moments before a critical pitch, and the poignant lessons learned from setbacks along the way. Emotions have colored every decision, reminding us that behind every business strategy lies a human story of passion, determination, and the courage to chase dreams.

As you close this chapter and look toward the horizon of what's next, remember the wisdom shared by those who've walked this path before. "Success is not final, failure is not fatal: It is the courage to continue that count," said Winston Churchill, capturing the essence of resilience in the face of uncertainty. Your journey has equipped you with a toolbox of skills—innovation, adaptability, and a relentless pursuit of excellence—that will continue to serve you well as you navigate the ever-evolving landscape of business.

Take a moment to thank your team—the unsung heroes who've fueled your journey with their dedication and unwavering support. Celebrate the mentors who've generously shared their insights, guiding you through uncharted waters with wisdom and grace. And above all, cherish the customers and clients who've entrusted you with their business, for they are the heartbeat of your success story.

As you embark on the next chapter of your entrepreneurial odyssey, remember that the road ahead may twist and turn, but with resilience as your compass and passion as your fuel, there's no limit to what you can achieve. Whether you're scaling new heights, pioneering innovative solutions, or simply savoring the fruits of your hard-earned success, may your journey be filled with laughter, learning, and limitless possibilities?

So, here's to you—the visionary, the risk-taker, the dreamer-turned-doer. Your story is a testament to the power of perseverance and the transformative impact of chasing your dreams. As you continue to write the next chapter of your entrepreneurial saga, may each page be filled with courage, creativity, and the unwavering belief that the best is yet to come.

GLOSSARY

- Accelerator: A program designed to support early-stage, growth-driven companies through education, mentorship, and financing.

- Angel Investors: Individuals who provide capital for start-ups, often in exchange for ownership equity or convertible debt.

- Bootstrapping: Building a business from the ground up with minimal outside investment, relying instead on personal savings and revenue generated from initial sales.

- Business Model: A plan or strategy implemented by a company to generate revenue and make a profit from its operations.

- Business Plan: A detailed document outlining a company's goals, strategies, target market, and financial forecasts.

- Competitive Advantage: The attributes or conditions that allow an organization to outperform its competitors.

- Crowdfunding: The practice of funding a project or venture by raising small amounts of money from a large number of people, typically via the internet.

- Customer Persona: A semi-fictional representation of an ideal customer based on market research and real data about existing customers.

- Ecosystem: The network of organizations, individuals, and resources involved in the development, production, and delivery of products or services in a particular industry or market.

- Entrepreneurship: The act of creating, managing, and scaling a business to achieve desired outcomes, often involving innovation and risk-taking.

- Exit Strategy: A planned approach to how an entrepreneur will sell their ownership in a company, either through an acquisition, merger, or initial public offering (IPO).

- Incubator: An organization that helps start-ups grow by providing services such as mentorship, office space, and access to investors.

- Innovation: The process of creating new ideas, products, or methods that bring about significant improvements or changes.

- Lean Start-up: A methodology for developing businesses and products that aims to shorten product development cycles and rapidly discover if a proposed business model is viable.

- Market Opportunity: The potential for a product or service to fulfill a need or want in a specific market, leading to business growth.

- Market Research: The process of gathering, analyzing, and interpreting information about a market, including information about potential customers and competitors.

- Mentorship: A professional relationship in which an experienced person (the mentor) guides another individual (the mentee) in their personal and professional development.

- Minimum Viable Product (MVP): A product with just enough features to be usable by early customers who can then provide feedback for future development.

- Networking: The act of interacting with others to exchange information and develop professional or social contacts.

- Pitch: A presentation where an entrepreneur seeks to persuade investors or stakeholders to support their business idea.

- Pivot: A significant change in strategy or direction for a start-up, often based on market feedback and learning from initial failures.

- Risk Management: The identification, assessment, and prioritization of risks followed by coordinated efforts to minimize, monitor, and control the impact of unforeseen events.

- Scalability: The capability of a business to grow and manage increased demand without compromising performance or losing quality.

- Start-up: A newly established business venture, typically characterized by a high degree of innovation and potential for rapid growth.

- Value Proposition: The unique combination of benefits and features that a company offers to its customers, distinguishing it from competitors.

- Venture Capital: A form of private equity financing provided by investors to start-ups and small businesses with long-term growth potential.

- Vision: A clear, inspiring long-term goal that guides an entrepreneur's strategic decisions and actions.

Chapter – II

- Break-even Analysis: A financial calculation that determines the number of products or services a company must sell to cover its costs.

- Business Model Canvas: A strategic management template used for developing new business models and documenting existing ones.

- Cash Flow Statement: A financial statement that shows the inflows and outflows of cash within a company over a specific period.

- Competitive Analysis: The process of evaluating the strengths and weaknesses of current and potential competitors.

- Customer Acquisition Cost (CAC): The cost associated with acquiring a new customer, including marketing and sales expenses.

- Customer Lifetime Value (CLV): The total revenue a business can reasonably expect from a single customer account throughout their relationship.

- Elevator Pitch: A brief, persuasive speech that outlines an idea for a product, service, or project, typically delivered in the time span of an elevator ride.

- Executive Summary: A concise summary of the key points of a business plan, often the first section read by investors.

- Financial Forecast: An estimate of future financial outcomes for a company, including projected income, expenses, and profits.

- Go-to-Market Strategy: A plan that outlines how a company will sell its product or service to customers.

- Income Statement: A financial statement that shows a company's revenue and expenses over a specific period, resulting in net profit or loss.

- Key Performance Indicators (KPIs): Quantifiable metrics that reflect how effectively a company is achieving its business objectives.

- Market Penetration: The extent to which a product or service is known and used by customers within a particular market.

- Market Segmentation: The process of dividing a broad consumer or business market into sub-groups based on shared characteristics.

- Marketing Mix (4 Ps): A framework that includes Product, Price, Place, and Promotion strategies used to market a product or service.

- Milestones: Significant events or achievements that mark progress in the development and execution of a business plan.

- Mission Statement: A brief statement that defines a company's purpose, core values, and primary goals.

- Revenue Model: A framework for generating income, detailing how a company will earn revenue from its business activities.

- Sales Forecast: An estimate of the amount of revenue expected from future sales over a specific period.

- Scenario Planning: A strategic planning method used to make flexible long-term plans by exploring different potential future scenarios.

- SMART Goals: Objectives that are Specific, Measurable, Achievable, Relevant, and Time-bound.

- SWOT Analysis: A framework used to evaluate a company's internal Strengths and Weaknesses, and its external Opportunities and Threats.

- Target Market: A specific group of potential customers at whom a company aims its products and services.

- Unique Selling Proposition (USP): The factor that differentiates a product or service from its competitors, highlighting its unique benefits.

- Value Chain: A series of activities that a company performs to create value for its customers, from raw material procurement to delivery of the final product.

- Vision Statement: A forward-looking statement that outlines what a company wants to achieve in the future.

- Working Capital: The difference between a company's current assets and current liabilities, indicating its short-term financial health.

Chapter – III

- Career Path: The progression of jobs and roles within a particular field or industry that an individual might follow during their working life.

- Core Values: Fundamental beliefs and principles that guide behavior and decision-making in personal and professional life.

- Flow State: A mental state of complete immersion and focus in an activity, often leading to peak performance and enjoyment.

- Hobbies: Activities done regularly in one's leisure time for pleasure and relaxation.

- Ikigai: A Japanese concept meaning "reason for being," representing the intersection of what you love, what you are good at, what the world needs, and what you can be paid for.

- Intrinsic Motivation: The drive to engage in an activity for its own sake, deriving satisfaction and fulfillment from the activity itself.

- Life Purpose: A deeply held sense of meaning and direction in one's life, often aligning with personal values and goals.

- Mindfulness: The practice of being present and fully engaged in the current moment, often used to reduce stress and enhance focus.

- Passion Project: A personal endeavor undertaken with great enthusiasm and dedication, typically outside of one's regular professional responsibilities.

- Personal Branding: The practice of marketing oneself and one's career as a brand, emphasizing unique strengths and expertise.

- Professional Development: Continuous learning and growth in one's career, involving acquiring new skills and knowledge to advance professionally.

- Purpose-Driven: Acting with intention and focus, guided by a clear sense of purpose and direction.

- Self-Discovery: The process of exploring and understanding one's own personality, values, skills, and interests.

- Self-Reflection: The practice of examining one's thoughts, feelings, and behaviors to gain insight and understanding.

- Strengths Assessment: Tools and techniques used to identify an individual's core strengths and talents.

- Vision Board: A visual representation of one's goals and aspirations, often used as a motivational tool to clarify and focus on what one wants to achieve.

- Work-Life Balance: The equilibrium between personal life and professional responsibilities, aiming for a healthy, sustainable lifestyle.

- Zone of Genius: The area where one's greatest strengths and deepest passions intersect, leading to exceptional performance and satisfaction.

Chapter – IV

- Angel Investors: Individuals who provide capital for start-ups at the early stages, usually in exchange for convertible debt or ownership equity.

- Bank Loans and Lines of Credit: Traditional financing options where banks lend money to businesses, either as a lump-sum (loan) or as a revolving credit line (line of credit).

- Bootstrapping: Funding your start-up using personal finances or operating revenues of the business.

- Cash Flow Management: The process of tracking how much money is coming into and going out of your business.

- Crowdfunding: Raising small amounts of money from a large number of people, typically via the internet.

- Exit Strategy: A planned approach to how an entrepreneur will sell their ownership in a company, either through an acquisition, merger, or initial public offering (IPO).

- Financial Fundamentals: Basic principles and concepts of managing finances, including budgeting, cash flow, and financial statements.

- Friends and Family Funding: Raising capital from friends and family members to fund your start-up.

- Grants and Competitions: Non-repayable funds or products given by one party, usually a government department, corporation, foundation, or trust, to a recipient.

- Investor Relations: Managing communication and relationships with investors to ensure they are informed and supportive.

- Profitability Analysis: Assessing the financial viability of a business by examining its ability to generate profit.

- Tax Planning and Compliance: Strategically planning your finances to maximize tax efficiency while ensuring compliance with tax laws.

- Venture Capital: Financing provided by investors to start-ups and small businesses with long-term growth potential.

Chapter – V

- Building a Positive Company Culture: Establishing a work environment that reflects the values, beliefs, and behaviors of the organization.

- Conflict Resolution: Methods and processes involved in facilitating the peaceful ending of conflict and retribution.

- Crafting Job Descriptions: Writing detailed descriptions of job duties, responsibilities, required qualifications, and reporting relationships.

- Delegating Effectively: Assigning responsibility and authority to others to complete tasks while retaining accountability for the outcome.

- Developing Leadership Skills: Enhancing abilities that help individuals lead, guide, and influence others effectively.

- Effective Recruitment Strategies: Techniques and approaches used to attract, select, and hire the best candidates for job openings.

- Encouraging Innovation and Creativity: Creating an environment that supports and nurtures the development of new ideas and innovative solutions.

- Identifying the Right Talent: The process of finding and recognizing individuals who possess the necessary skills, experience, and attributes for specific roles.

- Interview Techniques: Methods and strategies used to conduct interviews and assess the suitability of candidates for a job.

- Managing Remote Teams: Overseeing and coordinating the work of employees who work from locations outside the traditional office.

- Motivating Your Team: Techniques and practices for inspiring and encouraging employees to achieve their best work.

- Onboarding New Employees: The process of integrating new hires into the organization and equipping them with the necessary tools, knowledge, and support.

- Performance Management: The continuous process of setting objectives, assessing progress, and providing ongoing coaching and feedback to ensure that employees are meeting their goals and career development needs.

- Team-Building Activities: Exercises and activities designed to improve teamwork, communication, and collaboration among team members.

Chapter – VI

- Analyzing Marketing Metrics: The process of examining data related to marketing activities to gauge performance and effectiveness.

- Building a Community Around Your Brand: Developing a loyal group of customers and followers who actively engage with and support your brand.

- Building Your Brand Identity: Creating a unique image and personality for your brand that differentiates it from competitors.

- Closing the Sale: Techniques and strategies used to finalize a transaction with a customer.

- Content Marketing: Creating and distributing valuable, relevant, and consistent content to attract and engage a target audience.

- Crafting a Compelling Value Proposition: Developing a clear statement that explains how your product or service solves a problem, delivers specific benefits, and why customers should choose it over competitors.

- Customer Acquisition: Strategies and tactics used to attract new customers to a business.

- Customer Relationship Management (CRM): Managing a company's interactions with current and potential customers using data analysis to improve business relationships.

- Digital Marketing Essentials: Key components and strategies for promoting products or services through digital channels.

- Leveraging Influencers and Ambassadors: Utilizing individuals with a significant online following to promote your brand and reach a wider audience.

- Networking and Relationship Building: Establishing and nurturing professional relationships that can lead to business opportunities.

- Paid Advertising Strategies: Approaches for using paid media, such as online ads, to reach and engage potential customers.

- Public Relations: Managing the spread of information between an organization and the public to build a positive reputation.

- Sales Funnels and Lead Generation: The process of guiding potential customers through a journey from awareness to purchase.

- SEO (Search Engine Optimization): Techniques to improve a website's visibility on search engines like Google to attract more visitors.

- Storytelling for Sales Success: Using narratives and stories to create an emotional connection with potential customers and drive sales.

- Understanding Your Target Market: Researching and identifying the specific group of consumers most likely to buy your products or services.

Chapter – VII

- Beta Testing: The process of testing a product by real users in a live environment before its official release.

- Brand Alignment: Ensuring that all aspects of a product and its marketing are consistent with the brand's identity and values.

- Cross-Functional Collaboration: Teams from different departments working together to achieve common goals in product development.

- Idea Generation: The process of creating new concepts or solutions for products through brainstorming and creativity.

- Iterative Design: A cyclical process of prototyping, testing, and refining a product to improve its functionality and user experience.

- Market Readiness: The state of being fully prepared to introduce a product to the market, including aspects such as marketing, production, and distribution.

- Minimum Viable Product (MVP): A simplified version of a product that allows a team to collect the maximum amount of validated learning about customers with the least effort.

- Prototyping: Creating a preliminary model of a product to test and refine concepts and design features.

- Scalability Planning: Preparing for the growth of a product in terms of production, distribution, and customer support without compromising quality.

- User-Centered Design: An approach to product development that focuses on the needs, wants, and limitations of the end-users.

- Validation: The process of confirming that a product concept is viable and meets market needs through testing and feedback.

Chapter – VIII

- Automation: The use of technology to perform tasks without human intervention, enhancing efficiency and accuracy in operations.

- Customer-Centric Operations: Business processes designed to prioritize and enhance the customer experience.

- Lean Principles: A systematic method for waste minimization within a manufacturing system without sacrificing productivity, which can be applied to start-ups to improve efficiency.

- Logistics: The detailed coordination and implementation of complex operations involving the movement of goods, services, and information.

- Metrics: Quantitative measures used to assess, compare, and track performance or production.

- Risk Management: The identification, evaluation, and prioritization of risks, followed by coordinated efforts to minimize, monitor, and control the impact of unfortunate events.

- Scaling: The process of increasing the size and scope of a business's operations to handle a growing market demand without compromising quality.

- Supply Chain Management: The management of the flow of goods and services, including all processes that transform raw materials into final products.

- Customer Support Scaling: The expansion of customer support services to accommodate a growing customer base while maintaining service quality.

- Crisis Management: The process by which an organization deals with disruptive and unexpected events that threaten to harm the business or its stakeholders.

- Business Continuity Planning: Preparing for and managing the continuation of business operations during and after a disaster or unexpected disruption.

Chapter – IX

- Adaptability: The ability to adjust to new conditions and changes in the environment or circumstances.

- Continuous Improvement: An ongoing effort to enhance products, services, or processes by making incremental improvements over time.

- Feedback Loops: Systems where outputs of a process are used as inputs for future actions, facilitating continuous learning and improvement.

- Innovative Problem-Solving: The use of creative and unconventional methods to find effective solutions to challenging problems.

- Iterative Development: A process of developing a product through repeated cycles (iterations) of testing and refinement.

- Learning from Failure: The practice of analyzing failures to gain insights and improve future performance.

- Mentorship: Guidance provided by a more experienced person to support the personal and professional growth of a less experienced individual.

- Personal Resilience: The capacity of an individual to recover quickly from difficulties and adapt to adversity.

- Resilience: The ability of an organization or individual to withstand and recover from significant challenges and setbacks.

- Strategies for Overcoming Adversity: Planned actions and approaches designed to manage and overcome difficult situations.

- Support Networks: Groups of individuals or organizations that provide assistance and encouragement during challenging times.

- The Power of Resilience: The strength and capability derived from being resilient, enabling sustained success despite obstacles.

Chapter – X

- Adapting to Regulatory and Legal Changes: Adjusting business practices to comply with new laws and regulations.

- Anticipating Market Trends and Disruptions: Predicting changes in the market and potential disruptions to stay ahead of the competition.

- Building Resilience in Supply Chains: Creating a robust supply chain that can withstand disruptions and maintain operations.

- Corporate Responsibility: The commitment of a business to contribute positively to society and the environment.

- Diversifying Revenue Streams: Expanding the range of products or services offered to generate multiple sources of income.

- Embracing Remote Work and Hybrid Models: Adopting flexible work arrangements that combine remote and in-office work.

- Future-Proofing: Strategies and actions taken to ensure long-term success and sustainability of a business.

- Innovation as a Core Strategy: Integrating innovation into the fundamental approach to business operations and growth.

- Investing in Technology and Automation: Allocating resources to advanced technologies and automated systems to improve efficiency and competitiveness.

- Sustainability: Implementing practices that support long-term ecological balance and reduce environmental impact.

- Strategic Partnerships and Alliances: Forming collaborative relationships with other organizations to achieve mutual goals.

- Preparing for Economic Uncertainty: Developing plans and strategies to navigate and thrive during economic fluctuations.